The Stonebuilder's Primer

The
Stonebuilder's
Primer

A STEP-BY-STEP GUIDE FOR OWNER-BUILDERS

CHARLES LONG

FIREFLY BOOKS

A FIREFLY BOOK

Cataloguing in Publication Data

Long, Charles
        The stonebuilder's primer : a step-by-step guide for owner-builders

Rev. & expanded.
ISBN 1-55209-298-4

1. Stone house – Design and construction – Amateurs' manuals.
2. House construction – Amateurs' manuals.   I. Title.

TH1201.L65   1998   690'.8   C98-930996-7

Published in Canada in 1998 by
Firefly Books Ltd.
3680 Victoria Park Avenue
Willowdale, Ontario M2H 3K1

Published in the United States in 1998 by
Firefly Books (U.S.) Inc.
P.O. Box 1338, Ellicott Station
Buffalo, New York 14205

We acknowledge the financial support of the Government of Canada through the Book Publishing Industry Development Program for our publishing activities.

Produced by
Bookmakers Press Inc.
12 Pine Street
Kingston, Ontario K7K 1W1

Design by
Ulrike Bender
Studio Eye

Printed and bound in Canada by
Friesens
Altona, Manitoba

Printed on acid-free paper

Photography by Dan Maruska
Illustrations by Ian S. R. Grainge
Cover photograph by Bernard Clark

To Dorothy (McDermott) Long,
who built the foundations.

THE AUTHOR began building his house on a bedrock farm in eastern Ontario in 1975 and just couldn't stop. When the house was finished, he turned to stone paths, walls, outbuildings, fireplaces, even docks, and he was eventually seen tidying up some fallen masonry on the Great Wall of China. When the rocks run out, he works as a freelance magazine writer and television host. His other books include:

HOW TO SURVIVE WITHOUT A SALARY

THE BACKYARD STONEBUILDER

LIFE AFTER THE CITY

COTTAGE PROJECTS

UNDEFENDED BORDERS (a novel)

Contents

*Of course, stones want to fall—straight through the wall
beneath. Gravity helps to hold them all in place.*

I The Myth of Stone

Architecture is inhabited sculpture.

—Constantin Brancusi

FIELDSTONE IS AN IDEAL MEDIUM for amateur builders. The massive strength in solid walls of stone comes more from the material than from skill. And if the lines are not exactly straight, no critic's eye can tell which wiggles are the builder's and which of them came with the stone. Little mistakes can disappear in the rough-hewn texture of the rock.

Despite the forgiving nature of the material and its undeniable beauty, surprisingly few amateur builders are willing to tackle a homemade house of stone. Such reluctance is unfortunate because it is too often based on unfounded fears. As our own stone walls began to grow visible from the road, we attracted a steady stream of passing admirers and critics. The first was a real estate agent, teethed—no doubt—on stockbroker Tudor and relocatable anything. He watched for a while, then shook his head and muttered, "Gonna make a hell of a noise when it comes down."

Others have been more polite but no more confident in the capacity of two green exurbanites to raise a stone house from scratch. The doubts are usually voiced in one of three ways:

"What if it falls?"

"It must be more complicated than that!"

"That stuff must weigh a ton!"

Only the last of those doubts has any basis in reality. A house-worth of stone weighs more than a ton—it can weigh hundreds of tons. Taken one stone at a time, though, it is no more than any other middle-aged, out-of-shape weekend putterer could handle or, indeed, could benefit from.

"What if it falls?" is a fear that makes much less sense. Gravity ensures that every stone presses directly down on the ones beneath. Of course it wants to fall, but it wants to fall straight down through the other stones. It can't go anywhere unless some force pushes it sideways out of the wall, and such a force would have to be extremely potent to push out a stone that is held in place by tons of rock above. In reality, there might be a danger that a whole wall section would begin to tip in unison. Good foundations and a few simple design rules make such a catastrophe very unlikely.

"It must be more complicated than that!" is the usual comment of those who watch us work for a while or even try a hand themselves. The answer is, "It doesn't have to be." With the greatest respect for the professional

Traditional stone walls were built with two faces, often with rubble filling in the centers.

masons and engineers who design and build the truly complex jobs, I must distinguish such work from the very plain and simple skills that suffice to build an ordinary wall in an ordinary house. Real stonemasons are a rare and talented breed. Their skills take years to learn and develop. They have the ability to build airy spires, flying buttresses and fanciful designs that reach the limits of the material. A simple wall in a simple house, however, is the sort of thing that untrained yeomen and illiterate peasants have built for themselves for millennia past. It is only in this recent era of the specialist that we have begun to doubt our ability to do such simple things for ourselves.

Weekend builders don't hesitate to go after wood with hammer and saw, though few are master carpenters. Amateur painters abound, though professionals could do better. Why, then, should building with stone be any different? There is a myth about stone that makes newcomers disbelieve the ease with which they can create beauty and strength. "It must be more complicated than that." Of course it is, but even the most amateurish efforts are still capable of producing a house that will outlast anything made of wood.

A few years ago, we found ourselves living in a too-small house surrounded by fencerows and fields full of stone. Heartbreak and frustration for farmers but a bonanza for the builder. With the basic material so freely at hand, building in stone was an easy choice. The hard part was in deciding how. Full of all the doubts that our roadside critics later voiced, we set about looking for an easy way.

Blessed with an abundance of old stone buildings in the area, we found no shortage of examples of different styles from which to choose. Sandstone, limestone and granite abound. Fine houses and official buildings, the heritage of craftsmen who emigrated from Scotland 150 years ago, set a benchmark for skill and polish that we knew was beyond us. Cruder buildings, barns and cellars, obviously built by the settlers themselves, were clearly within the limited range of amateur talents we could muster but didn't seem up to the building code or up to our expectations of what a house should be.

Building with forms, the method first described by Edward Flagg, expanded by Helen and Scott Nearing and adopted by Karl and Sue Schwenke (*Build Your Own Stone House Using the Easy Slipform Method*), seemed, at first, to meet our needs. In the end, it proved to be more complex and expensive than were simpler, more basic techniques.

TRADITIONAL TECHNIQUES

To the casual observer, a wall of traditional stone construction may appear more neat and orderly than it really is. The closely fitted stones in the visible face are just that—a façade. Chances are, only a few of them extend through the full thickness of the wall. If you could walk inside and look at the back of the wall, you would not see the expected mirror image of the front but a whole different face. The two faces are tied together with a few large stones that reach from one side to the other, and the rest of the core is of rougher construction, rubble or even air space.

The two-faced approach is one of the reasons that older stone buildings have such massively thick walls. Accommodating the rough back sides of two faces meant that a wall could rarely be less than 2 feet thick. Some masons deliberately left air spaces in the core as the only concession to insulation. It worked—to a degree—but required an even thicker wall.

Even with air spaces in the core, lath and plaster, paneling, paper or anything else the shivering inhabitants were wont to add, early stone houses were cold and often damp as well. Modern renovators add new stud walls on the inside with a full thickness of insulation or resign themselves to leaving an oil truck backed up to the furnace all winter. With an inner lining of fiberglass and studs, the walls get thicker. And the inevitable result of thicker walls is smaller rooms—or having to start with a bigger house.

The bigger-house alternative brings us to the other disadvantage of the traditional technique: its extravagant use of material. The massive walls require more stone, and building two faces requires more of the better stones, the flat-sided ones or the carefully cut ones. When masons worked with teams of horses and underpaid apprentices to haul and cut the stone, such extravagance might have been warranted.

We, however, were set on going it alone. The two of us together weighed only 250 pounds, and we hardly had a callus between us. An 18-inch wall would weigh 80,000 pounds less than a 24-inch wall. A mere 6 inches would save us 40 tons of digging, hauling, dragging and lifting. And then, to keep us warm, the extra inside face would have to be covered anyway. It was hardly worth the effort.

THE SLIPFORM METHOD

Slipform building is virtually a poured concrete wall with stones set in the outer face. The builder begins with a large number of portable wooden forms that are bolted and wired together to contain the pour. After the forms are aligned and braced, stone is set in the front and concrete is worked between and behind them. When a section has set, the lower forms are unbolted, removed and replaced on top of the higher forms, leapfrogging up the wall.

This was at first appealing because it required only a single face of decent stones, backed with concrete and rubble. Ergo: thinner walls and 40 tons less wear and tear on the builders. Moreover, putting stone and concrete inside solid lumber forms assuaged our neophyte fears that anything we would build might well come tumbling down. Any dunce—or so we thought—could pour concrete around the backs of stones and leave it alone to become a wall. Its basic appeal was that it seemed so foolproof, and we were hardly aglow with confidence.

In truth, we never got to the concrete stage. The first stumbling block was the cost of the lumber needed to make all those forms. Then I reread the books and realized that the authors of slipform books invariably cut the lumber from their own forests. Enough said.

Not only is the lumber expensive, but changing, aligning and bracing forms seemed to consume about half the working time on a slipform job.

Finally, we were too late in noting the standard slipform advice to design straight walls in lengths that are convenient multiples of the length of the standard form. Our footings were already poured, committing us to fanciful nooks and turns—none of which were in convenient multiples of anything.

In a traditional wall, the flat sides of the stone are laid in the horizontal plane, leaving level courses.

We didn't even have a level surface from which to start. The footings were poured right on bedrock, rising and dipping in staircase sections over the irregular planes of subsurface strata. Faced with the expensive and time-consuming job of custom-building special forms for all those odd lengths of lower footings just to get a single level surface from which to start, we resolved to try hand-laying stone on the lower footings. It would be underground and thus invisible to later critics. There were no corners or fiddly bits in the lower sections. There seemed to be no risk in trying, at any rate. So we stretched some string for guidelines, slapped on a layer of mortar, a course of stones, more mortar . . .

Much to our amazement, the dips and valleys were brought up to grade in three short days—just what we had budgeted for building and fitting the special forms. Moreover, the outer face was considerably more presentable than what we had come to expect from the slipform method.

With a solid, level perimeter on which to build, we once more contemplated building forms. The expense was giving us pause. At that point, we were struck by what seemed to us an obvious saving: After the wall was complete and the last of the forms removed, we would still have to erect a separate interior wall to hold the wires and insulation. Why not build the interior wall first (or the frame, at least), use that as the basis of the inside forms and save half the cost of forming lumber? Why not, indeed?

So, on the inner lip of the foundation, we built an ordinary wall frame of 2-by-4 studs—the whole interior wall of the house. Half a sheet of particleboard set against the studs made an ideal inner form, and when removed, it left a ½-inch air space to later vent away any errant condensation.

We were still prepared to use forms on the outer face of the stone wall and proceed with a modified slipform approach. But the weather happened to be fine that week, and we knew we ought to save form building as a rainy-day-in-the-barn project.

Ever so cautiously, we troweled on a bed of mortar, applied a mosaic of stone and another layer of mortar and just kept going. We've put up more than 200 tons of fieldstone since that day and still haven't gotten around to building those forms.

To be fair, I suppose we really should try using slipforms, but frankly, it would seem a little retrograde—like going back to paint-by-number after finding you can make pictures more easily all by yourself.

Step by step, we evolved an approach to stonebuilding that combines features of both traditional and slipform methods. From the traditionalists, we kept the basic stone-on-stones approach that avoids all the fuss and bother with forms and wires and braces and bolts. From the slipform adherents, we borrowed the notion of building against a movable backboard, a shortcut that allows lazy builders (like us) to use all the best and biggest stones up front and shave heavy inches off the back.

Briefly, the method works like this:

1. The permanent wall framing of the house is built on the top of the foundation or footing.

2. The framing is kept to the inside edge of the foundation's top, leaving a wide outer base (12 to 24 inches) on which to build the outer wall of stone.

3. A temporary backboard spacer is placed against the studs at the back of the space where the day's stones will be laid.

4. A line is strung a given distance from the studs to define the outer edge of the projected stonework.

5. A bed of mortar is spread on top of the wall.

6. A layer of stone is seated on the mortar, aligning the front edges of the stone with the string and working in rubble and rougher pieces to fill the spaces against the backboard.

7. The layer of stone is brought up to a level top by filling any spaces with smaller stones and mortar.

8. Another bed of mortar is spread on top of the stones, and the next layer of stone (or "course") is begun at the face.

9. Later on, the outer face is pointed and finished.

10. The next morning, the backboard is pushed out of the space between the studs and the stone and is reset behind the new day's projected work, the string is raised to the higher level, and you're back to spreading mortar with a bare 10 minutes of preparation.

Subsequent chapters will expand on all these steps and deal with special problems and more complex jobs as well, but the basis of any house is the wall, and a wall of stone can be as simple as these 10 steps.

It's tempting to compare this method with veneer techniques. They do both begin with a basic stud-wall frame and add stone to the outside as a later step. Veneer, however, is merely decorative. The strength of the house is entirely dependent upon the wooden frame, which bears the weight of the roof and upper stories. Consequently, stone veneers are thin—as little as 3 or 4 inches in some cases.

Our own stone walls are a solid 16 to 18 inches. They hold up the top of the house and stand sturdily independent of the wooden inner walls. Howling gales may rattle the windows, but the solid stone wall never shudders in any storm.

Because inner and outer walls are independent, they can admit an air space between to prevent warm, moist inside air from condensing on the cooler stone and rotting the wood.

Apart from the obvious matter of immovable strength, the greatest difference between veneer and a real stone wall is in the final appearance. It is more than simply gauging the thickness of a wall by the depth of windows and other openings. It is the appearance of the stones themselves.

Stone that has been cut and quarried by natural forces may be left with a flat side or two, but the rest of its shape is likely to be quite irregular. In traditional building techniques, most of the stones would be laid on their flat sides, with irregular edges left to project from the face or be buried on the inside of the wall. The purpose was to simplify the task of matching rough stone to irregular spaces by trying to keep the courses level. Unusually good blocks might be set on edge, but most stones were placed with the flattest faces in the horizontal plane.

In a thin veneer wall, the flattest faces are placed in the vertical plane—either set flush to the frame of the building or exposed on the outer wall. The stones, in effect, are all set "on edge." The result is an appearance distinctly different from older, traditional solid-wall construction.

The photograph on the following page shows veneer and solid construction on the same building. The builder, the stone and everything else are identical, but

The chimney on the right is veneer at the base and solid construction above. Veneer has a different look, especially at the corner.

it is not hard to tell which is veneer and which is solid.

Unfortunately, the slipform wall—solid though it may be—usually gives the appearance of veneer. Because the form does not admit the knobs and projections of irregular faces, the temptation is to place the flattest side of the stone against the face form, leaving irregular rather than level courses. As a result, the stones appear to be set on edge, as they would be in a veneer. The slipform wall may be solid and attractive in its own right, but its modern veneerlike appearance is unmistakable.

Apart from its old-fashioned appearance, our compromise method has other attractions for the novice builder. Much of the worry in building your first house involves "the big mistake"—fear of committing some irreversible blunder, like sinking foundations, leaning walls or drains with no place to go. Pick your fear from the common litany of "things that go wrong when you don't know what you're doing." With all that time and money invested, blunders aren't funny, they're tragic.

In this method of building, most of the decisions from which the big boners spring are over before the first stone is laid. If your private terror is not getting

drains and foundations right, there's nothing wrong with having them poured professionally before you start. The proper placement and alignment of walls and openings are done at the framing stage. If there is a mistake, it can be found and corrected easily, long before the cement is mixed.

With the frame in place, all measures and levels are taken from it. There are no transits, marker stakes or temporary guideposts to worry about or knock out of place. If the frame is square and plumb, the stone walls that follow will stand straight too.

The novice is also well served by having only one face to build. The most skilled and time-consuming part of the job—selecting stones to fit—takes place mostly at the face. If that first big chunk doesn't fill the hole at the back, then a couple of smaller ones might, or at worst, a pail of concrete will fill just about any space. You wouldn't do that on a face, but back against a form, it works just fine.

Finally, the outer face, which is more carefully built (for looks as well as for strength), is open, visible and easily accessible. In a slipform job, the mason works blindly—from behind. He can't see the face he's building until the form is taken off two or three days later, when the concrete is set and it's too late to correct mistakes. Leaving the face open lets the builder rely on his eye rather than memory for important tasks, like keeping

A crude jumble of stones, a boulder and a wall. The builder's job is to arrange the elements in the vertical plane with level courses and overlapping joints—and an eye, of course, to aesthetic balance.

a roughly level course, avoiding continuous vertical joints and aesthetically balancing the size, shape and color of stones that show on the face.

Working on an open face is easier, too, in one final respect. Pointing (the outside finishing of the mortar joints) is quickly and easily done when hand-laying stone. It can be as simple as running a wet finger around the joints at the end of the day. When the work is done in a form, however, pointing has to be finished later, when fresh mortar must be tediously worked into cracks that have already set.

I've never seen another house built just like ours, but all the same, I'd be surprised if these shortcut ways to traditional style were in any way unique. For a long, long time, ordinary farmers and untrained folks have been laying up fieldstone houses and barns. The techniques and the styles have been as individual as the people with the trowels.

The surprise is that so many modern builders seem reluctant to try the job. It is, I suppose, modern man's trust in the competence of technology and degrees that leaves us doubtful about our own innate abilities. For some, the simplest task cannot be attempted without an evening course or a how-to book to provide the technological crutch. With all due respect to Flagg, the Nearings, the Schwenkes and others, the literature has done little to dispel the unwarranted mystique that has attached itself to the simple art of building in stone.

That alone is the reason for this little volume. The method expounded is a hybrid of others' inventions and would hardly be worth the paper to explain it—except for the fact that it is simple and it works.

The purpose here is to take some of the mystery and engineering mumbo jumbo out of what, it should be remembered, is one of the oldest, most basic and natural forms of building, one that predates any building code.

One well-educated man I know felt ignorant enough of the technical complexities of stonebuilding that he decided to get a professional contractor for a fairly small masonry job. He approached the most competent and highly regarded contractor around—a father-and-son team with many fine stone projects to their credit. My friend described what he wanted and asked for an estimate. Father and son proceeded to calculate the job requirements right on the spot, which led to a terrific family spat over the product of 8 times 7. Father and son were each so sure of their answers that it nearly came to blows. Wisely, my friend decided not to intervene with his suggestion of 56 as a third possible answer. The job was done—beautifully—and my friend had no more illusions about the technical skills required to achieve a fine result with stone.

Building in stone is, in some respects, a little like a garden. Just about anybody can grow a garden, and few would hesitate to try. Undoubtedly, a biochemist or agronomist, armed with computer models, testing labs and research results, could grow a superbly efficient garden. But that doesn't mean that the rest of us have to get a degree or hire an agronomist in order to have a garden.

With straw hat and hoe, we're not much improved on our ancestors, scraping the earth with pointed sticks. Agribiz chemists can outproduce us every time. But I'm not about to put astro turf on the garden and go back to supermarket tomatoes just because someone else is more expert than I.

By the same token, I can tip my hat to the skill of the professional artisans and the undeniable advantage of engineering tables—and go right on laying stones in my own crude way, not because it is better but because it is simple and basic and I like it.

Choosing a site with stones close at hand saves labor and ensures that the building will fit the natural landscape.

II Plans

If the design of the building be originally bad, the only virtue it can ever possess will be signs of antiquity.

—John Ruskin

BUILDING WITH STONE, like making babies, is one of those delightful tasks where the easiest part comes first. Planning a stone house can be done in the shade or around a cosy fire with a glass of something to oil the imagination. No aching backs and blisters—yet. Enjoy.

The usual planning considerations will get short shrift here. It is important to get the drains going downhill instead of up, to put the solarium on the sunny side and to angle the roof so that all the snow isn't dumped in front of the doorway. All those things, and hundreds more, pose problems that each home builder will have to solve somewhere else. The issue here, however, is stone.

The use of stone involves some problems unique to that material. Those are the problems which we'll consider here. The debates over where to put the septic tank and the proper size for a kitchen are not unimportant, they're just not in this book.

CHOOSING A SITE

You could, I suppose, build a stone house just about anywhere. Remember, though, that the hardest part of the job will be moving the stone to the site. You may find, like Mohammed, that it is easier to move yourself to the mountain than the other way around. If you have a choice, look for a site that already has a good supply of stone nearby.

Finding a rocky site is not as hard as it might seem. In agricultural areas, the cheapest land is usually the shallow land—a thin layer of soil over bedrock. Look for fieldstone piled along old fencerows or heaped in the middle of fields by frustrated plowmen. Hilly country offers ledges and outcroppings of ready-to-quarry material. Fast-moving streams bare rocky strata.

If nature won't provide, look for stone in the footsteps of man. Old, abandoned barns and homesteads often leave good stone foundations and cellars behind. Locating near former quarries, mines or heavy construction sites may offer access to blasting refuse, scrap stone or even a workable ledge.

Still stumped? Soil surveys or geological survey maps for your area will show you just where the rock sticks out of the earth. These maps may be obtained through libraries or agricultural representatives.

Finally, you can always find the stony ground by asking those who make their living in it. Well drillers, excavators and pole contractors (installing power and telephone poles) can give you a firsthand account of what lies under the surface just about anywhere.

In general, fieldstone prevails where bedrock lies close to the surface. Time, weather and the plow break off chunks of bedrock and bring them to the surface, where they become a perfect nuisance to everyone but you. Chances are, then, that a rocky building site not only provides a handy source of material for the stonebuilder but also solves potential foundation problems by offering the prospect of building directly on the bedrock. Bedrock provides a sounder base than any human-made foundation could.

Shallow soil is not without its problems. You may have to forgo a full-size basement or a septic tank, unless you're prepared to truck in dirt to cover these underground facilities. You may not be able to plant a tree just anywhere, and digging a root cellar might be tough. But these problems are not insurmountable. The security of having that heavy wall of stone safely borne by bedrock makes the choice of a bedrock site desirable.

Besides security, bedrock provides more flexibility for heavy interiors. Flagstone floors, hearths and inside stone walls can be added at will, with no concern about weight problems.

In our case, it was luck—not planning—that put us on a building site where bedrock was waiting just under the grass. Bad luck, some would say, but if I had to do it over again, I would look for another spot just like this one. And this time, it would be on purpose.

PLANNING THE HOUSE

With the site picked out, it is time to invest in a thick pad of squared (graph) paper and start designing the layout. A common approach is to design from the inside out. That is, start with decisions on how much space you need, how the space will be used and functional relationships (pantry beside the kitchen and toilet near the sleeping area, for example). When the space is arranged to your satisfaction, draw a wall around it. Or you may want to set up the design with passive-solar criteria in mind, orientation on the site itself, the relationship to the landscape or alignment with the planet Mars.

Whatever the approach, stone will impose additional design criteria. These include:

1. Minimizing the volume of the wall;
2. Minimizing the height of the wall;
3. Planning door and window openings that are narrow or extended to the roofline;
4. Avoiding long, straight walls.

The volume of the wall matters only because the darned stuff can weigh 150 pounds a cubic foot or more. If that doesn't make an impression, consider this: The most efficient enclosure is a round one. That is, you

Where bedrock lies close to the surface, the stones are a nuisance to everyone but the builder.

can enclose more space with less wall in a circle than in any other shape. Let's design an imaginary house with 1,200 square feet of floor space, enclosed by a wall 8 feet high and 18 inches thick. A circular design would require about 110 tons of stone; a square layout would take 125 tons; and a rectangular house (say, 60 feet by 20 feet) would need 144 tons. The rectangle takes an extra 34 tons of stone to enclose the same floor area as the circle. Think about it. Then curb the urge to give every room a southern exposure with skinny rectangles zigzagging along the slope.

The height of the wall matters for a similar reason. When we were working on our own walls at the waist-high level, it was no problem to take a stone from the wheelbarrow and drop it into the mortar. When we were 10 or 11 feet in the air, that little job took two of us and a complex system of ramps and scaffolds. At the top of a 20-foot chimney, every little 30-pound stone became an ordeal. Lower is better.

Lower walls can also be thinner, resulting in a smaller volume of stone. It is not very useful to generalize on just how thick a stone wall should be. That obviously depends on the quality of the stone as well as the mason. A 12-inch-thick wall made of flat-sided blocks will inevitably be sounder than the same-size wall made of round stones. For what it's worth, our building code allowed a 12-inch stone wall up to 36 feet high. We planned 16-inch walls up to 12 feet high and made the higher walls 18 inches thick. There were no scientific reasons for those dimensions, however. It simply suited the shape of the stones we were using (the biggest blocks we could handle would not have fit in a thinner wall). And it suited our self-confidence as builders to be well on the safe side of the prescribed limits.

Door and window openings are critical only if you

intend to continue the stone wall above them. There are a number of ways to do this (see Chapter VIII), and to my mind, there are few features of a stone building more satisfying than a well-built arch. However, regardless of whether the opening is capped with an arch or a lintel, the weight of the stone above it will demand a fairly narrow opening. Our workshop contains an arch with a 6-foot span. It is as solid as the smaller ones, but it was much more nerve-wracking to build. If your needs include patio doors or a bank of bay windows, count on filling in the space above them with wood, or extend the opening up to the roofline. Narrow arches are stronger and easier to build than wide ones are.

Long, straight walls are a practical advantage in slip-form building. They are also weaker than walls with turns, corners and fanciful nooks. The reason is simple. Try to stand a playing card on its edge. Now fold it once across the middle, and stand it on edge again. Every turning (or fold) gives the wall another "leg" that extends beyond the narrow base of the footing. Using this principle, amateur architect Thomas Jefferson found that "serpentine" walls were stronger and more efficient than were straight walls. A straight wall had to be at least two bricks thick. The serpentine wall was stronger, even though Jefferson built it only one brick wide. The long, straight wall is in no danger of falling as long as the base is wide enough, the wall is properly built and it is reinforced against flexing. But a crooked wall achieves the same strength with less material.

The official word on crooked versus straight calls for "lateral supports" in a solid masonry wall, spaced no farther apart than the thickness of the wall multiplied by 20. A 1½-foot-thick wall, for example, should have a lateral support every 30 feet.

These four basic design criteria (avoiding long buildings, high walls, wide openings and straight lengths) are all concerned with getting the most from the least amount of material. "Square, short, narrow and crooked" won't conjure up awe-inspiring visions among architects. But then, architects don't have to lift the stones or pay the cement bill. By all means, ignore these basics if square, short, narrow and crooked do not satisfy your needs. But do recognize that there will be a *quid pro quo*.

Compromise is inevitable. A dogleg in a long wall makes it stronger and allows it to be thinner, but it does require another complete set of cornerstones, which are harder to find than are ordinary wall stones. Narrow openings make it easier to span the gap above them, but bigger openings cut down on the amount of stone required. The compromise may be smaller windows but more of them. Low walls are easier to build than high ones, but a 2-story house will be cheaper to heat than will a sprawling bungalow (and it takes less roof to cover it). Our compromise was to plan a 1½-story house and

Rocky outcroppings, or ledges, are a handy source of stone. Roots and weather quarry a forest ledge.

accept the necessity of sloping ceilings upstairs.

Dream homes ought to come from dreams. But just before you wake up, go over those plans and add up the weight of stone in the walls. It's a simple calculation:

Length of wall x Thickness x Height = Volume

If you've measured everything in feet, the volume will be in cubic feet of stone and mortar. Multiply that by 150 pounds per cubic foot to find the weight of the wall. Then remember that each stone will be lifted several times: loading, moving, sorting, fitting . . . . That sort of reality may lead to a few compromises in the dream.

GETTING DOWN TO DETAILS

When the dreaming and sketching have been done to everyone's satisfaction and when the inherent constraints of stone have made their amendments, then it is time to transform art and vision into the nitty-gritty of practical working drawings, done to scale and including all the pipes and supports and chimneys and stairs and details that we ignored in Round One. Just to see whether all those dreams will fit together without the staircase ending in the bathroom or an

The practical details of chimneys, doors, stairs and supports require careful working plans, drawn to scale.

THE STONEBUILDER'S PRIMER

essential vent passing through the upstairs hall.

Here, I have an embarrassing confession to make. At this point, where vision gives way to practicality, Liz and I faltered and actually hired an architect to draw the plans for our own dream home. He did a lovely job. The plans are still around somewhere. We dig them out every once in a while and have a good chuckle over the folly of builders (albeit amateurs) asking nonbuilders (albeit professionals) to draw a plan for something as basic and personal as a house. Those who lift the stones make more practical houses than those who draw them. The plans, of course, bear absolutely no relation to the house that resulted.

The first few times, we were actually embarrassed about deviating from the "official" plan. When we realized that the deviations worked better than the plans did, we went back to stubby pencils, squared paper and something to lubricate the imagination. The end result we planned ourselves, much of it while the work was in progress. The only regret is having wasted the initial fee on a professional.

All the professional advice a reasonably handy amateur needs can be found in a copy of the local building code. In Canada, the National Research Council issues a booklet called *Residential Standards*, which is the basis of most local building codes. It is well laid out and easy to follow. In it, you'll find information on how wide doorways should be, the minimum elbowroom for a toilet, span tables for floor joists, acceptable ceiling heights, stair dimensions, and so on. It is an invaluable reference when the time comes to draw your plans to scale. The nearest CMHC (Canadian Mortgage and Housing Corporation) office will have copies.

OTHER POSSIBILITIES

Interior planning is the same whether you are building in stone or bamboo. A stone house requires only that you plan on thicker walls and pay homage to the four constraints mentioned earlier. Stone does, however, suggest some optional features that you may want to consider at this stage.

Stone fireplaces are attractive and not too difficult for amateurs when built around a prefabricated steel form. When planning a fireplace, consider the footings under it (again, bedrock is better) and plot the placement carefully so that the chimney will not interfere with the floors above. It is also useful if the chimney passes through the roof at a point near the peak. It "draws" better and is less likely to lead to a leaking roof than is a chimney placed at the eaves of a house.

Where there is no basement, it is a fairly simple matter to plan on flagstone floors. We have one under the woodstove and another one in the mudroom (if you have young children, you'll understand how appropriate the name is). Liz objected at first, having chilled her feet on stone floors in Britain. But we worked out a way of insulating them and would certainly include them again in other buildings.

Interior walls of stone are attractive (if done with restraint) and have at least two other functional advantages. As support walls, they are sturdy enough to withstand a regiment of square dancers or several 6-year-olds on the floor above. Placed near a window or stove, an interior stone wall can absorb and store a tremendous amount of heat. The wall keeps radiating warmth long after the sun has set and the fire has died away. It is important to separate interior and exterior walls so that the heat is not conducted away to the outside, but this is easily done.

Finally, the thickness of stone construction has the happy result of leaving broad, solid windowsills around the house. Plan on using these as window seats, mini-gardens and nooks. Our bathroom sink is built into a wide tiled sill. Another dormer sill makes a built-in desk with a view. These are features that seem to belong to a stone house. Don't overlook this opportunity to exploit the unique—even the eccentric—possibilities.

Chapters IX and X deal with these special features in more detail. At this point, the main concern is to get them into the plans—or at least leave the options open. You may find, as we did, that stone features which seem to be beyond your skills at the beginning will be child's play after you have practiced on a hundred tons of wall.

HOW LONG WILL IT TAKE?

There is little question that working in stone is one of the slower ways to get from vacant lot to finished house. It also takes longer for a stone house to crumble into a vacant lot again—a rationalization that won't make the walls rise any faster but might make you feel better about it.

The most time-consuming part is gathering and hauling suitable stone. So "how long" depends largely on how far you are from the source of material. By all means, though, do start the job *before* you gather up a house-sized pile of stones. Deciding what is a usable rock and what is a heavy piece of junk becomes considerably easier after a few weeks of fitting them into the wall. Gathering stone as you work results in a much smaller discard pile. Also, it is easier to select stones from a small array spread over the ground than from a mini-mountain where the best ones are always on the bottom.

Once we got the hang of it, Liz and I worked to a fairly routine quota of finished wall. On a normal day, we could expect to finish 30 cubic feet of masonry. In other words, a wall 20 feet long and 18 inches thick would grow 1 foot higher between morning and evening chores. It really did take two of us to maintain that pace, however. The usual division of labor required one of us full-time at the wall, spreading mortar, selecting, trimming and fitting stone. The other half of the team was kept busy mixing mortar and hauling more stone from the adjacent fields and fencerows. That pace didn't leave much time for coffee breaks, but it did allow for wiping noses, gardening, parenting and a yarn with the occasional roadside critic. In case you are wondering, it was Liz who was usually stuck with the mixing, hauling, nose wiping, et cetera. Which is why this book is dedicated to her. Visitors usually assumed, wrongly, that the one with the trowel was doing most of the work.

So if you have a hardworking partner and a supply of stone nearby, divide the volume of your walls by 30 to get a rough idea of the time involved. Add a couple of weeks to get the hang of it, adjust the estimate to allow for rainy days and freezing temperatures (when work must be postponed), and increase the total by 15 percent for every child under the age of 10—20 percent for 2-year-olds.

Obviously, that not-very-scientific computation addresses only the time involved in the wall itself. Foundations, framing, roof and all the less interesting bits of building will take more time. How much more time depends on how complicated your plans are and on too many other things for a generalization to be possible.

There are a few ways to speed up the action on the masonry front. Flat-sided stones are easier to fit than lumpy ones are. Hand-mixing mortar and hauling water consume inordinate amounts of time. I was tempted to avoid mentioning such things as being too patently obvious. Then I remembered that when we started, we often selected boulders with interesting shapes that just cried to be included on aesthetic grounds. It wasn't until later that "interesting" came to mean "easily fitted." Likewise, we started by hand-mixing mortar and carrying water in buckets from the well. Only later did we compromise on purist notions of the simple life and invest in a mixer and running water. If these tips are already obvious to you, then you are already smarter than we were when we started building in stone.

PLANNING AROUND THE WEATHER

Two elements can spoil a stonemason's day or at least slow it down considerably: freezing temperatures and rain. Apart from personal discomfort, freezing affects the use of mortar, the bond between the stones, the mixing, everything. It is possible to work in the cold, but the chances of doing a decent job are greatly reduced. When winter sets in, cover the unfinished wall with a tarp and plan on doing something else until spring.

It is easier to protect the job from excess water than from cold. Rain is just harder to predict. Plan to be prepared for it with tarps to keep the materials dry

and with your sturdiest covers ready to protect any wet mortar. Yes, it is the *wet* stuff that must be kept out of the rain. Forget the hardened mortar—rain is a positive benefit there. It is the fresh mortar that rain might wash out of the joints or turn so sloppy that it won't set properly.

In addition to keeping tarps on hand, we learned a few other lessons about being prepared that might save others a headache or two.

Setting up the sandpile is a good place to start. You will be mixing all the mortar right beside the sandpile, so keep it as close to the building as possible. Leave just enough room around the walls to move the scaffolds along. Putting the sandpile any farther away than that means unnecessary miles of carrying heavy mortar to the wall. Lay out some logs or sturdy boards to contain the edges of the pile. Otherwise, that nice, neat pyramid of sand will soon be 40 feet across and 6 inches deep. Also, cover the bottom of the future sand heap with a sheet of old plastic, tar paper or anything to keep the weeds from growing up through it. For some reason, weeds seem to prefer the expensive, imported sand to the domestic dirt all around them. Keep the expensive stuff for yourself.

Cats are almost as bad as weeds in a sandpile. All the more reason to keep it tightly covered with a tarp when not in use. Even then, our cats were waiting in line with their legs crossed when we came out to pull the cover off the sandpile each morning. Get a dog.

If there is any slope to the land at all, site the sandpile so that the first rain doesn't wash it away. Then plant the mixer on the *down*slope side of the pile. It is easier to shovel sand downhill into the mixer, and any erosion will move the sand closer to you rather than farther away. More important, at the end of every day, you'll be sluicing out the mixer with cascades of gloppy water. Better to dump it downhill, *away* from the sand heap.

One other precaution that will save time and effort is planning to have the backfill (replacing the dirt around the foundation) completed before you start building up the walls. You'll have more room to work and a better surface on which to maneuver wheelbarrows, scaffolds and the ever-present clutter of stones.

"How much?" depends on where, how big, how fancy and how much you're prepared to do yourself. For a normal house with insulated frame walls on the inside, building in stone should make no appreciable difference in cost. Most of the money will still be tied up in foundations, roof, lumber, floors, wiring, plumbing, insulation, interior finishing, et cetera. The additional costs to do it in stone will include sand, cement and a wider foundation. The stone itself, we'll assume, is free. The only saving to offset these extra costs is the outer covering of the normal frame house—the siding.

Calculating the cost of the masonry must start with

The most laborious and time-consuming part may be the gathering and hauling of enough suitable stone.

the volume of the walls. It also involves some guesswork to decide how much of that volume will be stone and how much will be mortar between the stones. Obviously, your skill in fitting the stones closely together will have a great effect on the mortar bill. Fat joints take more cement; thin joints take less. Using big stones requires fewer joints; smaller stones require more. For what it's worth, our own average was one bag of cement for every 10 cubic feet of wall. The basic wall was about 100 feet along the perimeter (after subtracting doors and windows), had an average height of 12 feet and was 16 to 18 inches thick. Its volume, then, was:

$$100 \times 12 \times 1\frac{1}{2} = 1,800 \text{ cubic feet}$$

For us, that meant buying approximately 180 bags of cement. The total cement bill would be close to $1,200 in 1998 prices.

Mortar, of course, takes more sand than it does cement. If bought in quantity, however, the cost of sand is negligible. In most cases, delivery will cost more than the sand itself. The bulk of our sand was taken from a pit 17 miles away. Haulage was charged from the company yard 10 miles away. For under $200, we bought enough of the highest-grade masonry sand available to build the entire house. For smaller jobs, we take the half-ton truck to the yard ourselves and get it loaded to the gunnels for $10.

How much will it cost to build a stone house? About as much as the same house built of wood. Stone takes a great deal more labor but little or no extra money.

A stone building is cheaper only when most other materials can be omitted—in other words, when insulation and inner walls are irrelevant. In a garage, a woodshed or a storage building, freestanding stone walls and a stone or earthen floor can be built with a few dollars' worth of sand and cement. Add a roof, and you have a cheap and solid building. You won't want to spend the winter in it, though.

One final note on the subject of costs. Budget-minded builders commonly negotiate prices for all materials before the job begins, asking suppliers to quote lower bulk rates for the entire job. A great idea, but don't make the mistake of accepting delivery of a couple of hundred bags of cement at the beginning of the job. No matter how carefully you store it, the powder will turn to lumps before you get the mixer broken in. Get a quantity price, but arrange to pick it up fresh—as you need it. You'll soon learn, too, the value of loading your own cement at the building-supply yard. Picking up the bag is the best way to tell whether the contents are powdery fresh or not.

The greatest cost to work in stone is time. Lots of it. Months and months to build a wall that could have been covered in a day with particleboard and vinyl siding. For that reason, perhaps the most critical preparatory step at the planning stage is not technical, not financial, not physical, but mental—accepting the certainty that quality won't be hurried. If you must have deadlines, make them generous ones . . . and enjoy.

*A foundation bears the weight of the building and acts as
a dam to keep the yard from pushing its way inside.*

III Footings & Foundations

The best preparation for good work tomorrow is to do good work today.

— *Elbert Hubbard*

OUR FIRST ATTEMPT to build a house in the country started with an old log place that had been thoroughly colonized by groundhogs, bats and dry rot. It was so derelict that the neighbor insisted the only sensible way to renovate was to use kindling and a match. Optimism (or naïveté) stopped us short of arson, but we did decide that it would be easier to move the house away from the bat manure than vice versa. And so we pulled the walls apart with the intention of reassembling them on a new foundation, 100 yards upwind.

The old "foundation" came as something of a shock. The bottom logs had been leveled (sort of) with one medium-size stone at each corner. Our pioneer predecessor had excavated a small cellar under the kitchen and piled the dirt around the outside of the walls. That was it! More than a century of frost, damp and burrowing vermin had reduced the bottom course of logs to pulp.

Determined to do a better job than that, I hired a big machine with an operator to excavate the new site. The evening before the big dig was to start, we drove out to pick a spot and set the stakes. The weeds were chin-high, the twilight was nearly gone, and the mosquitoes were getting fierce. We knew we ought to align the walls with the sun, keep the trees between us and the winter winds, check the drainage, sample the soil, measure the distance from the hydro line, keep close to the barn, far from the road and—above all else—stay well upwind from Ontario's largest deposit of bat guano. Of those important criteria, not one remained by the time we had walked across the field. There were only mosquitoes, weeds, the fast-approaching gloom and now the sounds of the baby crying from the back of the car. We settled on the first big clump of trees we came to (it was too dark to see that they were dying elms), pushed in four corner stakes in the lee of the trees and made a run for the car.

Bright and early the next morning, about the time I figured the work might be getting under way, I drove out again to see that all was going according to plan. The machine was idle.

"Just getting here?" I asked the operator.

"Just finished," he grinned.

I looked around for a pile of dirt, but there was nothing to be seen over the weeds. I followed the tracks across the field to where the stakes had been placed. They were still in position, the four corners joined with a tidy little ridge of dirt, and there in the middle was a bedrock

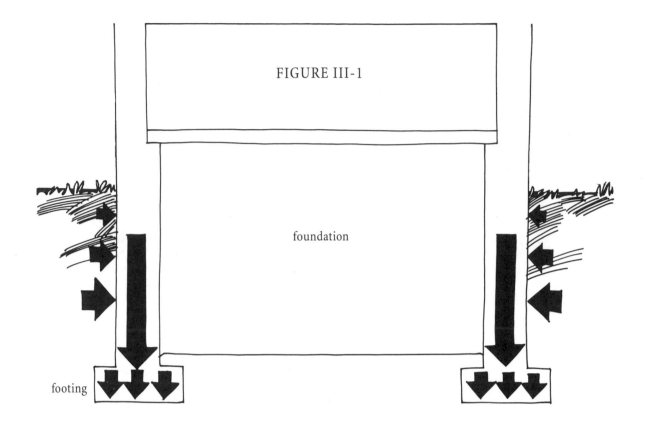

FIGURE III-1

foundation

footing

floor—one easy step down from the edge. I could have excavated the whole damned pit with a stable broom in the time it took to write out the check for the heavy equipment.

Terrible planning, but a stroke of luck to salve all of our amateur uncertainties over foundations. We erased the basement from the plan and set about building on bedrock. Still, it seemed too easy like that—about as technically sophisticated as rolling up four big stones on which to rest the corners. So we checked and rechecked and finally concluded that even the most cautious building code would allow a building many times heavier than ours to stand here with little more preparation than brushing the soil off the stone.

Obviously, that kind of security has more to do with luck than with planning. So let's assume that some builders will face the more complex problems of building on dirt, where the security of bedrock is too far down to find. What then?

Footings and foundation walls have functions that are quite distinct, despite my tendency to lump the two together as the underground parts that hold up the rest of the house. As Figure III-1 illustrates, the footing acts as, well, it acts as a foot. It distributes the weight of the wall over a wider surface in the same way that a snow-shoe distributes the weight of a walker. The weight of the building bears down vertically through a footing, but the important dimension is the horizontal area.

A foundation, on the other hand, is simply the underground part of the wall. Like any other part of the wall,

it must be sturdy enough to bear the compression of the weight above it. But the critical force is the lateral one. Like a dam, the foundation wall has to hold back the weight of earth trying to push its way in from outside. As well, it must withstand the inner pulling and tearing forces that result if the footings sink too far or—worse still—begin to sink unevenly.

Understanding these forces helps to make some sense of the complex rules that govern such matters in the building codes. The object of all the technical jargon in the rules is mostly to ensure that the footings are wide enough to carry the weight and that the foundation walls won't buckle.

There are three basic questions involved in footings: How deep? How wide? How thick?

How deep? Deep enough to get down into "stable" soil and well below the frost line. Unstable soil is the changing upper layer, where organic material is decomposing, roots are moving through the soil and freezing/thawing/soaking/drying actions shrink and expand the earth. Those natural movements in the earth's upper levels may seem benign to us, but they are hell on buildings, particularly buildings made of things like stone that will crack before they bend with these tiny flexes. Water, for instance, expands as it freezes. That minuscule expansion can lift the side of the biggest stone house—and drop it again with the thaw. It's those tiny movements which will gradually crack the wall.

Your building inspector will tell you the depth of the frost line in your locale. Do remember, though, that

FIGURE III-2

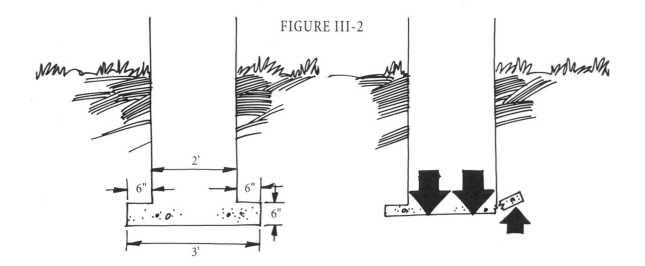

these are only averages and are affected by other factors—the depth of the snow cover, for example. So if you are planning a driveway beside the house and intend to keep the snow cleared off, that uninsulated section of ground will freeze more deeply than the rest. A good reason to place the footings *well* below the frost line.

As for the rest—the worm, root and compost action—just keep digging until you run out of evidence of living things, somewhere in the subsoil. The darker topsoil is good for gardens, bad for footings. This is a good time, too, to keep a watchful eye out for tree roots and clay deposits. Wet clay shrinks considerably as it dries, causing the house to settle and shift uneasily. In the wrong soil, one long dry spell is enough to crack foundations. Tree roots can invade a foundation, cracking it directly. Or—in a dry season—a big tree can draw moisture from the soil unevenly and crack foundations with the resulting soil shrinkage.

When you have managed to dig your way past all those potential problems, then that is deep enough for the footings.

How wide? The wider the footing, the more weight it will bear. So the place to start is with a rough calculation of the building's weight. Start with the stone walls. Length multiplied by height multiplied by thickness equals the volume of the walls. Subtract the volume of window and door openings. Assume the stone and mortar will weigh about 150 pounds per cubic foot. That gives the weight of the masonry. Now you should estimate the weight of the inner walls, the grand piano, lots of active visitors, floors, roof and all the snow on it. But that is too complicated even for the pros. A common shortcut is to calculate the total area of the floor and roof and estimate the weight at 100 pounds per square foot. And that, by the way, is very generous on the side of safety. That weight, plus the weight of the masonry, is the total weight that must be borne on those underground snowshoes.

Example: Imagine a house 30 feet wide by 40 feet long. The walls, including the foundation, are 15 feet high and an average of 1½ feet thick and contain no doors or windows. The total length of the walls (140 feet) times the height (15 feet) times the thickness (1½ feet) gives a volume of 3,150 cubic feet. That much masonry (at 150 pounds per cubic foot) will weigh about 472,500 pounds. The floor area (30 feet by 40 feet) is 1,200 square feet. At 100 pounds per square foot, that is 120,000 pounds. The roof, let's say, is 1,800 square feet, putting another 180,000 pounds in the weight column. The total weight of the house: 772,500 pounds. Remember the in-laws are coming, and round it off to an even 800,000 pounds.

We have the weight, but there is one other side to the question: the nature of the soil on which the footing will rest. Soils that are already compact will not be compressed much further by the weight of a well-footed wall. In loose soils, the building will need a wider footing to avoid that sinking feeling. If you can't tell the difference between sand, clay, shale and gravel, by all means have the soil tested. A building inspector, agricultural representative or even a friendly contractor will give you an idea of the basic class of the goods. If you steer on the safe side of the weight limits, a general idea of soil type is enough.

Builders should recognize that conditions vary from place to place, and local practice is usually a safer guide than generalization. However, just to illustrate the role of soil type in the design of footings, consider that our code allowed these bearing weights on common soils:

compact sand	3,000 pounds/square foot
compact silt	2,000 pounds/square foot
firm clay	1,500 pounds/square foot*

*These limits are for buildings of three stories or less, with under 6,000 square feet of ground area.

In the previous example, we imagined a house 30 feet by 40 feet with a perimeter 140 feet long and a total weight of 800,000 pounds. The stone wall was 18 inches thick, which means that the bottom of the foundation

FIGURE III-3

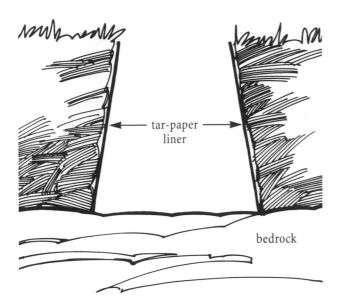

In firm soil, concrete can be poured into earthen forms.
A wooden lip helps level the top.

wall rests on the top of the footing with a pressure of about 3,800 pounds per square foot.

$$\frac{800,000 \text{ pounds}}{140 \text{ feet x } 1.5 \text{ feet}} = 3,809 \text{ pounds/square foot}$$

That would be too much pressure even for compact sand. Widening the bottom of the wall with a footing spreads the same weight over a larger area. A footing 2 feet wide would reduce the pressure to 2,700 pounds per square foot.

$$\frac{800,000 \text{ pounds}}{140 \text{ feet x } 2.0 \text{ feet}} = 2,857 \text{ pounds/square foot}$$

That footing would support the house on compact sand, but not on finer silt or clay soils. To meet the limit

for firm clay (1,500 pounds/square foot), the footing would have to be 3.81 feet wide.

$$\frac{800,000 \text{ pounds}}{140 \text{ feet x } 3.81 \text{ feet}} = 1,499 \text{ pounds/square foot}$$

In practice, few amateur builders are that precise or that fussy about stinting on material. My ruler doesn't have 3.81 feet on it. I would call it 4 feet and feel marginally more secure. Likewise, in mixed soils, if you are unsure whether there is more sand or clay in the dirt, call it clay and use the more cautious limit.

Having decided how deep and how wide the footings must be, it remains only to settle on a proper *thickness*. Some guides say 4 inches minimum, others say 6 inches. The most sensible rule, though, is that a footing should be thicker than its projection beyond the wall. Figure III-2 shows a foundation wall 2 feet wide, resting on a footing 3 feet wide. That leaves a 6-inch projection on either side. So the footing should be at least 6 inches thick. A thinner footing risks breaking off the projection.

FILLING IN FORMS

When the excavation is deep enough and the safe dimensions of the footings calculated, it is time to prepare for the pour.

The final digging should be done with great care, for the footing should be poured on *undisturbed* soil, which means that filling in the low spots to level the base is frowned upon. The loose soil will eventually compact and weaken the base on which the footing rests. Better to lower the high spots than to raise the low spots.

In some soils, the final dig might even eliminate the need for lumber forms. We happen to have a firm, sandy soil with just enough clay in it to hold it together. Cutting foundation trenches very carefully with a spade

THE STONEBUILDER'S PRIMER

Concrete is worked into the forms with a shovel to spread it and to work out any air pockets.

leaves a smooth-sided ditch from sod to bedrock. We line the sides with tar paper to keep out the dirt and to leave a smoother face on the concrete. The bottom of the ditch is carefully cleaned, and the concrete is poured directly into the earthen "forms." Sometimes a board is added at the edge to form a level top in uneven ground (see Figure III-3). For the house—where parging, damp-proofing and level surfaces were more critical—we avoided the shortcuts and stuck to carefully set lumber forms. But the outbuildings were all raised on these "formless" foundations and have shown no ill effects.

If lumber forms are your choice, remember to brace them securely. The weight of wet concrete against the sides will try to force the forms apart, even bowing the boards. Pieces of scrap nailed across the top, from one side to the other, will help to keep it in shape.

Finally, just before the concrete arrives, stockpile lots of odd-shaped rocks (no need to waste the good ones) all along the outside of the forms. Grab a shovel, and you are ready to pour.

At this point, there is always some temptation to make the concrete ourselves in the little backyard mixer. Every time we've succumbed to that temptation, we've come to regret it. The problem is that critical pours, like footings, ought to be done in a single day. Stretching it out in smaller doses—adding fresh concrete to yesterday's hard stuff—results in a much weaker product. There is a limit to what the backyard mixer can make in a day and a limit to the amount of mix we can move around without collapsing into jibbering blisters by evening. Now we call in the truck for the big one-day jobs and save our energy for other tasks.

Regardless of who supplies it, the concrete is poured into the forms and vigorously chopped about with a shovel to work out the air pockets and settle the mix into all the spaces. At the same time, we drop the stockpiled rocks into the settling concrete, being careful to leave plenty of concrete between them. Our original purpose for adding the rocks was to displace concrete, filling up space with free rocks rather than with expensive concrete. Later, we learned that the bigger rocks, left sticking up above the top of the forms, were not a mistake but an essential piece of the business. Buried half in the footing and half in the foundation wall, these boulders function as a tie between the two. They keep the wall attached to the footing. Building codes refer to this as a "key," and although contractors usually do the job with reinforcing steel rather than with boulders, the purpose is exactly the same.

Working on bedrock is somewhat simpler. In fact,

FIGURE III-4

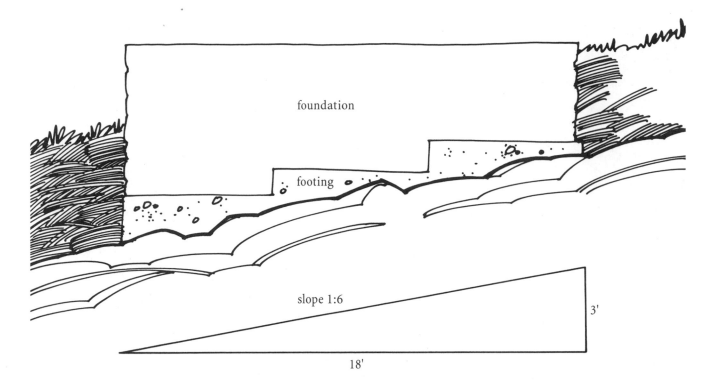

foundation

footing

slope 1:6

3'

18'

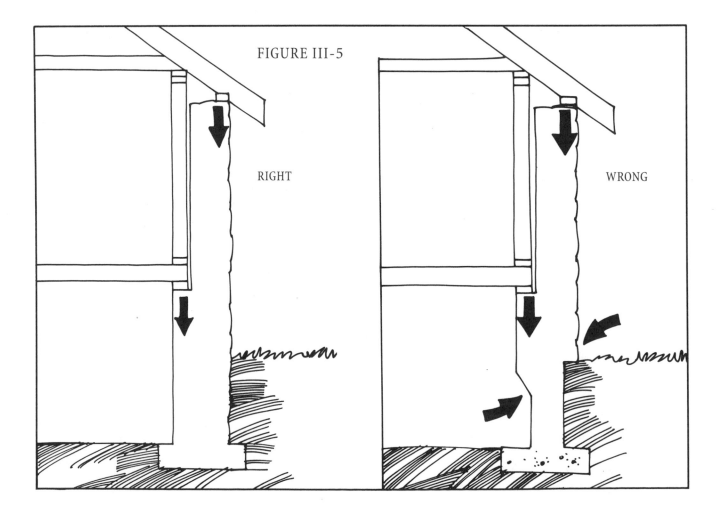

FIGURE III-5

RIGHT

WRONG

it is perfectly acceptable to start building the foundation wall right on the rock—without pouring a footing at all. We, however, usually do pour a footing, simply because it is a convenient way to establish a level base on which to start the masonry. Prepare the forms, just as you would for any concrete pour, then clean the bedrock surface with a wire brush. All the dirt and loose particles should be removed.

The only potential problem on a bedrock site might be the slope. If the rock surface slants by more than 1:6 (a 1-foot drop over a horizontal distance of 6 feet), the footing should be keyed to the bedrock. Lay out the footings so that they cross over natural projections or depressions in the surface, or break a few chunks of rock out of the surface to create a depression. A solid footing, extending into these holes, will keep the building from slipping down the slope (Figure III-4).

Footings are such an unsatisfying part of the job. Mentally, I can accept how critical they are, but it does seem counterproductive to begin by burrowing down into the earth, lowering what was already there. Buildings ought to rise. From this point on, they do.

FOUNDATIONS

The foundation, remember, has two main functions: carrying the weight above it and holding back the press of earth and water all around. The foundation wall is designed with these two functions in mind.

Bearing the weight is best accomplished by putting the heavy parts directly over the foundation (Figure III-5). In this way, the major force at work is the compression on the stone. The wall will fail only if the weight succeeds in squeezing your stones into flatter shapes or crushing them. Most unlikely! However, if the weight is allowed to bear down *beyond* the faces of the foundation, the forces act in a twisting way that can succeed in tearing a wall apart.

With that in mind, the foundation wall should be made at least as thick as the thickest part of the wall above it, and thicker still to hold the sill plates on which joists or beams will rest. If you are planning a stone wall 16 inches thick, with a 1-inch air space, and a supporting ledge for floor joists (set on a 2-by-4 sill plate), then the foundation should be at least 21 inches thick:

16 inches + 1 inch + 4 inches = 21 inches

The other stress arises from the yard's desire to be in the basement. Since the tendency is to push the walls *in*, building codes call for lateral support at the top of foundation walls. A stone wall on top of the foundation counts as lateral support. So do floor joists, which are anchored to the top of the foundation with bolts. In other words, don't worry about lateral support for the foundation—if you are building with stone, you've already got it.

Residential standards developed by the National Research Council prescribe minimum thicknesses for foundation walls. Naturally, the standard depends on how much dirt is outside trying to get in. A poured concrete foundation 12 inches thick will hold back 7½ feet of earth (measured from the basement floor to the top of the lawn). A masonry wall 12 inches thick will hold back a 7-foot height of earth. Most stone foundations must be more than 12 inches thick just to carry the wall above them. The standard, therefore, is usually surpassed in any solid stone construction.

When you know how high and how thick the foundation wall should be, you are ready to start building it. I suppose one could choose to pour a concrete foundation on the premise that most of it will be invisible underground anyway. The chief deterrent is that the forming will be far higher, and therefore more complex, than that involved in the footings. Where we had to use lumber to form the footings, they were mostly one board high. We nailed them together at the corners, leveled, squared and braced them and called for the concrete truck. If the foundation is several feet high, however, it will require a much more solid form to hold the concrete.

A masonry foundation, on the other hand, can be started with no more preparation than setting corner stakes and stringing lines to keep the faces rising vertically. Chapters VII and XI will offer some suggestions on how to lay up such a wall. There is, however, no substitute for a few frustrating days spent with trowel in hand trying to fit square rocks into round spaces—and vice versa. In other words, even if the process could be described perfectly, most readers will repeat many of the mistakes that most of the rest of us make in the beginning. Which is why I like the idea of starting with masonry rather than concrete foundations: I buried all my learner's mistakes, and by the time the walls rose above the ground, the stonework was beginning to look a little better. Put your practice work down where only the worms will notice.

A HOLE IN THE WALL

Whether you pour or mortar the foundation, you will have to make provisions for some holes through the wall. Most houses will require things like floor drains in the basement, an exit for sewage or wastewater pipes, an opening for the water supply, windows for full-size basements, vents for an unheated crawl space and access to cellars and crawl spaces.

Where the various pipes have to pass through the foundation, leave an opening slightly larger than the pipe. Granted, it may be easier just to bury the pipe itself in the masonry, but such shortcuts are much regretted later, when the pipe springs a leak or has to be removed for any reason.

A broomstick mortared into a joint leaves an air vent (TOP). *Larger vents* (BOTTOM) *are built like windows.*

The easiest way to leave a hole in the wall is to bury a short length of larger-diameter pipe. For example, our water supply from the well had to pass through a section of poured concrete. When the form was ready, we fitted two drainage tiles end to end; they extended neatly from one side of the form to the other. The concrete was poured around them, and when the forms were removed, there was a 4-inch hole left in the wall. This single hole took a 1¼-inch line from the well, a ½-inch copper pipe carrying pressurized water from inside the house to an outside tap and a small plastic air hose to vent the well. When all the bits and pieces were in place, I squirted in some expanding foam to fill the spaces around the smaller pipes and keep the groundwater out of the house. Sure enough, the very next year, the 1¼-inch line sprang a leak. We pulled it out, fitted a new one and resealed the passage with a minimum of fuss.

For other utility passages, we have used short sections of plastic pipe mortared into the wall. Stones beside the pipe, more mortar and a bigger stone across the top finish the job neatly.

The small holes that vent the air space between stone walls and studs were made with a broken broomstick— a piece 1 inch in diameter and about 2 feet long. We wiped it all over with grease and fitted it into joints between the stones. We took care to see that the outer end was lower than the inner end (so any condensation would drain to the outside), then built more wall above it. The stick was left in place until the mortar was set. Slick with grease, the broomstick pulled out easily and left a tidy 1-inch hole through the wall. We bought 1-inch soffit vents at the hardware store and stuck these in the outside end of the holes to screen out pests.

Larger vents, or hatches for the crawl space, are built in just like windows. In fact, these openings provide a good place to practice on smaller arches before you get to the big ones over the real windows.

SETTING THE SILL PLATE

The final bit of built-in business on the foundation comes at the top, where the anchor bolts are set to hold the plate. This is the point where the foundation narrows to become the wall per se. The resulting ledge supports the floor joists and framing. It is possible (and acceptable under some building codes) to mortar the ends of the joists right into the wall. The problem is that the wood will rot before the stones do, and the poor fellow who has to replace the joists will curse the builder who would take such a shortcut. Use a ledge and a plate. A plate will also make it easier to level the joists.

Get the big bolts—at least 8 inches long and ½ inch in diameter, with an L-shaped hook at the end. You will need at least two bolts for every length of 2-by-4 in the plate and no more than 8 feet between bolts. Set the string at the level where you want the top of the finished ledge to be. The final course of stones should stop just shy of that height. The hooked ends of the bolts are set in place during the laying of the final stone course. If possible, turn the hooks so that they stick under the edge of a stone. Line them up so that the shaft is about 2 inches in from the edge of the wall (to pass through the *center* of the 2-by-4 plate), and set them high enough to leave 2 to 3 inches of bolt above the string (Figure III-6).

When the mortar around the bolts has hardened, lay out the 2-by-4s along the ledge, mark the position of the bolts and drill some generous holes. Staple a length of sill gasket to the underside of each board. Now spread a bed of fresh mortar on the ledge, slip the 2-by-4s over the bolts, and tap them with a hammer to settle them into the mortar. Thread on the washers and nuts, and wrench them down until the plate is level and in position. If the string is still in place, you can use that to line up the plate.

FIGURE III-6

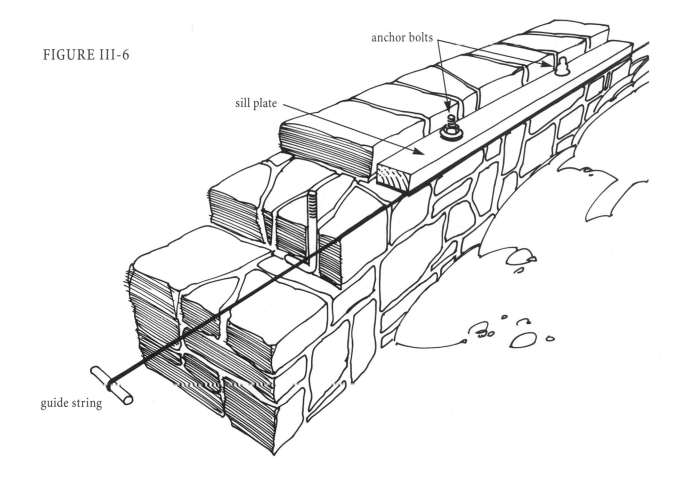

anchor bolts

sill plate

guide string

Any lumber used in the plate should, of course, be treated against rot. Rot is also the reason for the sill gasket, a thin foam strip that prevents moisture in the masonry from touching the wood.

The foundation is not complete until it is sealed. With paint or a piece of chalk, walk around the outside of the building drawing a contour line on the wall where the earth will be backfilled against the foundation. Everything below that line will be underground and should be "parged." This is particularly important if the foundation has a rough stone face.

Mix up a big batch of sticky mortar. One scoop of Portland cement, 2 scoops of masonry cement and 8 scoops of sand will work. Get the wall slightly damp, and start slapping on the mortar. Work it thoroughly into all the joints and depressions. A big, flat trowel will help to plaster it out to a smooth surface. Start at the footing, and work your way up to the line—all around the outside of the building.

When the parging is dry, you will need some "foundation coating" and an old broom with which to spread the tarlike substance on the walls. This time, start at the line, and work the goop down the walls and right over the footings.

The drains (clay tile or perforated plastic pipe) are laid beside the footings and led away from the house in trenches (headed downhill, needless to say). Six inches of gravel or crushed rock goes over the drains, then a layer of plastic or tar paper, then the dirt. The purpose of the plastic is to keep the dirt from filtering through the gravel and plugging the drains with silt. Now take all the rest of the dirt you've been tripping over for months, and push it back against the foundation. The earth should slope *away* from the walls to help the drainage.

Waterproofing can get quite fussy. I suppose that is inevitable if you are going to put a rec room in the basement with carpets on the floor. But if you just want somewhere to stow the potatoes, the only necessary step that remains is to spread sheets of plastic on the floor, under the slab if you're having one. If it is only a crawl space, throw enough sand on the plastic to hold it down and get on with the rest of the building.

Whether you're building a tree house or a stone house, a framework of wooden bones will shape the space.

IV Framing

In creating, the only hard thing's to begin;

A grass blade's no easier to make

than an oak.

—*James Russell Lowell*

THE WOODEN FRAMEWORK that forms the skeleton of the modern house has a number of vital functions. These lumber bones support the weight of floors, walls, ceilings and (in some cases) the roof. They hold the doors and windows; they hide the insulation, wiring and much of the plumbing; they form the interior walls, and (in our case) they guide the building of the exterior walls.

When building with stone, the exterior wall and support for the roof don't depend on the framing. All those other necessary functions remain, however. Without a skeleton of some kind, a stone house can be little more than a shell—a thick, empty skin.

The apparent complexity of framing comes about because builders want that single set of bones to perform all of those functions and they want it done with as little lumber as possible. The complications are mostly visual, however. Once the builder has made a few basic choices, the rest is largely common sense and reference to the local building code.

If the budget becomes a factor in framing choices, be wary of false economies. Quality materials, like kiln-dried lumber and galvanized spiral nails, add a small percentage to the overall cost of a house.

CHOICES

The basic choices facing the framer/mason are: how thick to make the inner walls, the best spacing for the studs (the vertical wall members) and when to lay the subfloor.

The thickness of the walls, or the width of the lumber in the frame, is mostly a matter of how much insulation you want. The common 2-by-4 stud (which is really only 3½ inches wide) will hold enough fiberglass to provide insulation with a value of R12. A wall of stone, an air space and drywall paneling on the inside will add precious little insulation—R2 at the most. In contrast, the highest standard in new homes is R20 in the walls. To meet that new criterion, modern builders add foam-board panels to the outside of a 2-by-4 frame or switch to a 2-by-6 frame with fiberglass alone (6 inches of fiberglass is rated at R20).

We used both 2-by-4s and 2-by-6s in the house. The thinner 2-by-4 walls were mostly around areas where closets or cold storage created an extra dead-air space inside the walls. Walls that enclosed living space and the nearly blank back wall that faced the northwest winds were framed with 2-by-6s and insulated with

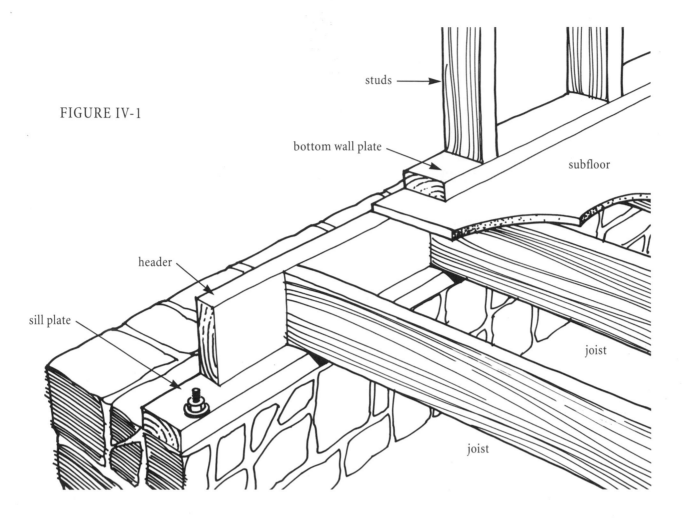

FIGURE IV-1

studs

bottom wall plate

subfloor

header

sill plate

joist

joist

R20 fiberglass. The workshop was framed mostly with the cheaper 2-by-4s (knowing that the volume of scrap from amateur woodworking will be more than enough to keep the heater blazing).

Whether you choose 4-inch lumber, 6-inch lumber, fiberglass, foamboard or a mixture of everything, just remember that building the outer walls of stone will shield the house from chilling winds. It will moderate temperatures by storing heat in its mass (slowing down the effects of sudden changes in the outside temperature). It will protect you from arrows, hailstorms and marauding Visigoths. But stone will *not* insulate worth a damn. Put the insulation in the frame.

Having chosen the width of the lumber, you must make a related decision on spacing. Generally, builders space joists, studs and rafters 12 inches, 16 inches or 24 inches apart. The measure is taken from the center of one stud to the center of the next, and the jargon is 12, 16 or 24 "oc" (on center). These standards are chosen for no other reason than the fact that each divides evenly into 48 inches—the standard width of the plywood or Gyproc sheets that are usually nailed to the frame. Spacing studs to any of these standards ensures that sheets will always join on a stud, where they can be nailed.

Choosing the spacing isn't entirely arbitrary. Closer

spacing is stronger, wider spacing weaker, and the building codes dictate maximum spacing for various weights to be supported. For example, in our local building code, an exterior wall that supports a roof, attic storage and one floor can be framed with 2-by-4s on 16-inch centers. Our own roof was supported on stone, but we stuck to the accepted practice of framing 2-by-4 walls on 16-inch centers and switching to 24-inch centers where the walls were framed with 2-by-6s. Check your own building code for allowable spacings. Aside from what is allowable, there are two other criteria: Wider spacing uses less lumber and is therefore cheaper, and narrow spacing provides more nailing support for inside walls.

Finally, the floor. On a normal framing job, the procedure would be to bolt the sill plate to the top of the foundation (Figure IV-1), fasten the floor joists and header to the plate, then lay out the subfloor. The wall frames can then be assembled flat (laid out on the subfloor), raised to an upright position, plumbed and braced. It can be done just like that in a stone building too, but remember that it may be months (or longer) before the amateur mason is ready to roof it over. In the meantime, that plywood subfloor is getting soaked. The surface will ripple, crack and splinter.

The alternative would be to omit the subfloor at the

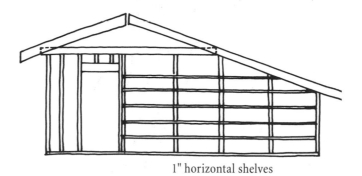

1" horizontal shelves

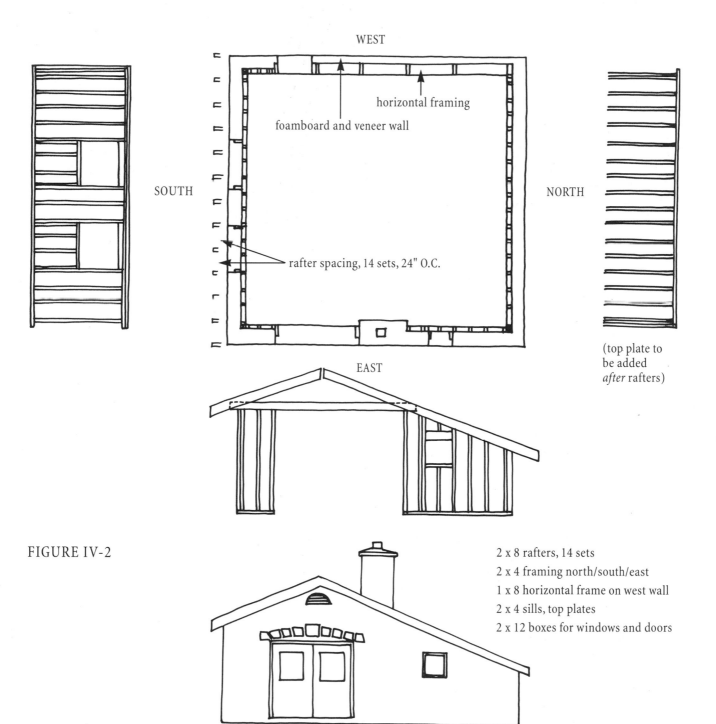

WEST

horizontal framing

foamboard and veneer wall

SOUTH

NORTH

rafter spacing, 14 sets, 24" O.C.

(top plate to
be added
after rafters)

EAST

FIGURE IV-2

2 x 8 rafters, 14 sets

2 x 4 framing north/south/east

1 x 8 horizontal frame on west wall

2 x 4 sills, top plates

2 x 12 boxes for windows and doors

framing stage, assembling the walls as best you can without a solid surface on which to work. The walls would be raised directly on top of the joists, and the subfloor added later, after the roof is on. You would have to add extra header blocks between the joists so that the subfloor could be supported at the edge; but the real disadvantage is the inconvenience of trying to work without a floor inside.

We chose the conventional route, knowing it would result in a rough subfloor that would have to be covered with the finished flooring sooner rather than later. When we added the second subfloor for the upstairs, we covered it with a monster sheet of plastic as a makeshift "roof." Both floors, however, still got wet and ragged before the real roof was in place. Even so, a little water damage was a small price to pay for the advantage of having floors from which to work.

When you have decided on your framing approach, draw a picture of it. Nothing fancy. The sort of thing you see in Figure IV-2. It helps to have top views *and* side views. Then add up the amount of lumber in the plan, add a percentage for wastage, and phone your friendly lumberyard.

Framing is not as complicated as it looks. Trying to draw a plan of the whole house at once put me on the verge of another panic call to an architect. Fortunately, the panic passed. I drew the floor, then the downstairs walls, with top and side views:

- studs evenly spaced;
- a stud at the side of every opening;
- a stud in every corner (for nailing), even if you have to squeeze in an extra one;
- one bottom plate;
- double plate on top;
- lintels above the openings set "on edge."

That much was simple and straightforward. I stopped while I still understood the plan, ordered only that much lumber, built it and ignored the second story and the roof until the stone walls were 8 feet high. It was a coward's approach, but it worked. When we were ready for the rest of the frame, I drew another floor (for the second story) and another set of walls. When the stone was finished to the rafter plates, we drew a final framing plan for the roof. Like any unfamiliar fare, building plans are easier to digest in smaller bites.

Working in easy stages does, however, leave lumber piles sitting idle for undue lengths of time. Our original pile of green, construction-grade spruce twisted itself into a shambles of corkscrews and warps before we were halfway through it. I complained to the lumberyard about the quality of their product and was given some kind advice, without the slightest hint that the builder might be as green as the lumber. "My friend," said the merchant, "unless you can get her all nailed up on the day she arrives or spend the extra money on the kiln-dried stuff, anybody's lumber is going to warp. The only way to keep it from curling is to cover it up with a tarp." That sounded like a load of cod's wallop to me, since it couldn't possibly get any wetter than it already was, and I said so.

"Oh no," he laughed, "it's not the wet that warps it—it's the sun! It's the sun drying out the top side faster than the bottom side that warps it. The trick is to keep it shaded." I tried it. It works.

THE SILL PLATE

You prepared for the sill plate earlier by leaving all those anchor bolts sticking up from the top of the foundation. The sill plate is simply a line of 2-by-4s laid flat along the inner lip of the foundation to form a resting place for the floor joists. Drill through the boards where they have to fit over the top of the bolts, check to see that they fit, then take them off again.

If the top of the foundation is level, roll out lengths of sill gasket, punch some holes for the bolts and put the gasket on the ledge *under* the sill plate. The idea is to stop dampness from rising through the foundation and into the wood. For the same reason, the sills should incorporate lumber that has been treated against rot.

If the top of the foundation is not level, the sill should be laid in a bed of mortar. And again, keep a strip of sill gasket on the underside of the plate. Now add washers and nuts to the anchor bolts, and cinch them down until the plates are level. Let the mortar harden before setting the joists.

FLOORS

Check the span tables in your own building code for the accepted size and spacing of joists. We used 2-by-8s on 16-inch centers, which permitted a span of up to 12 feet. Part of the kitchen was wider than that, so we added an intermediate concrete pier under the floor to support the longer joists in two shorter spans.

The ends of the joists are set on the sill, spaced properly, nailed to the sill and to a "header" board nailed across the ends of the joists. Short block headers can be nailed in the spaces between the joists to keep them from twisting, or smaller boards can be nailed in an X-shaped brace for the same purpose.

Now nail down the subfloor on top of the joists. Remember to start the edge of the sheets right at the outside edge of the header so that the wall plate will be evenly supported under its full width. Also remember, if you are using tongue-and-groove plywood, that these sheets are exactly 8 feet long but are less than the expected 4 feet wide (to allow for the tongue). The plywood is laid *across* the joists. A friend started to lay his subfloor along the joists and soon found that the edges

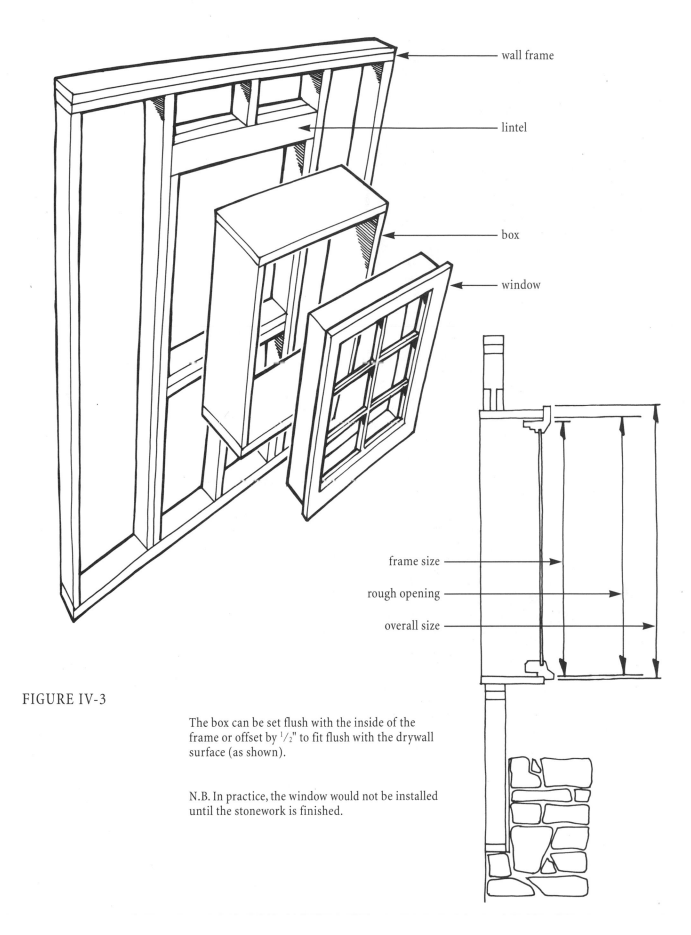

wall frame

lintel

box

window

frame size

rough opening

overall size

FIGURE IV-3

The box can be set flush with the inside of the frame or offset by $^1/_2$" to fit flush with the drywall surface (as shown).

N.B. In practice, the window would not be installed until the stonework is finished.

of the sheets were refusing to meet on the joists.

Chalk lines across the plywood at 16-inch intervals will make it easier to hit the joists with the nails.

WALLS

With subfloor down, you are ready to frame a wall. Lay the lumber out on the floor, with all the boards on edge. First the bottom plate, then the studs at right angles to it and, finally, the top plate. Use the pattern of plywood in the subfloor to help get the framework square. Mark the top and bottom plates to show the stud spacing, keeping them 16 inches or 24 inches on center.

We will worry more about doors and windows later. For now, it is enough to leave openings boxed into the studs. See Figure IV-3 for an example of this layout. Notice that the lintel over the opening is framed with two pieces, each with a face left flush with the rest of the frame. Also, the drawing shows two studs on either side of the opening, the inner stud supporting the lintel. That is the approved method for conventional framing. Since we will be adding a box and tying the whole thing into the masonry, strength will not be a problem. Finally, these framed openings should be made at least 3 inches wider and 3 inches higher than the "rough opening" called for in the window specifications.

With all the elements in place, start nailing the whole thing together. Not too tightly—one nail per joint is enough for now. Chances are, the hammering has knocked something out of square, so square it up again and double-check the measurements. Now get some long boards (scrap will do), and nail them diagonally across your masterpiece. That will brace everything into a rigid panel until it is up and joined to the other walls. With the temporary brace secure, you can finish nailing the thing together.

Only after the wall section is completely assembled do you call for some helpers. Tip the wall up into position, slide it around until the bottom plate is lined up properly with the edge of the subfloor, then hold it there in a more or less vertical position while one of the helpers nails a few sturdy props into place. Voilà! A wall.

The next stretch of wall, which joins the first one at the corner, is assembled on the floor and raised in a similar fashion. The two sections are then carefully plumbed and nailed together at the corner. If we were building an ordinary frame house, we would nail plywood sheathing to the outside of the frame at the corner. The plywood would serve as a permanent brace, holding the frame in square and plumb. Our stone walls, however, will hold the frame in place at the corners and at every door and window opening. Omit the plywood corners, and leave the temporary diagonal braces on.

With the frame walls up, we started laying stone. We could have just as easily added the second-floor joists

Door openings, like windows, are rough-framed as boxes that project from the stud wall into the masonry.

Rough openings for windows can be framed with an open "box" of 2-by-12 lumber. The box is slipped into the opening left between the studs (LEFT). A groove is scored around the box to form a masonry key. As the masonry is laid around the box (RIGHT), the key helps to seal the junction between masonry and wood.

and tented the whole thing over with a tarp. In a one-story building, you could add the ceiling joists to support a tarp. But the walls alone are enough to get the mixer started. Adding more of the upper frame at this stage is useful only if you want to cover the job more securely against the weather. Just don't get carried away and frame up roof and rafters too. Remember that the rafters will rest on the stone.

WINDOWS AND DOORS

Framing these openings requires more precision than we used with the rough-and-ready approach to the rest of the wall. It doesn't require more skill—just a more careful approach to measuring and fitting.

We've used brand-new prefabricated windows, recycled windows, adapted old storm windows from the dump, homemade doors and even one window made from the cast-iron top of an antique butter churn. The

principles are the same for all. However, let's begin with the simplest case, and assume that you're starting with new prefab windows.

Most manufacturers describe their window wares with these standard measures: overall size, frame size, rough opening and glass size (nice to know but irrelevant for planning the framing). Each of these measures is given in the length and the width. Figure IV-3 shows the cross section of a typical factory-built window. Casement windows, horizontal and vertical sliders, awning windows and other types all move the glass around in different ways, but the window frame is all that matters here, and the frames are all similar to that shown in the drawing on page 39.

"Overall size" will be of some importance later, when the masonry is built up around the box. The window itself will not be installed until the stonework is finished, and the masonry will have to be kept far enough back from the edges of the opening to avoid interference with the outer flanges of the window. Overall size is measured to the outer edge of these flanges, or trim. It is meant to be larger than the opening.

The "frame size" refers to the window frame, not the frame of the house. This is the part of the window that fits into the opening of the box.

The "rough opening" is the size of the hole you must leave for the window. Don't be confused by the fact that

FIGURE IV-4

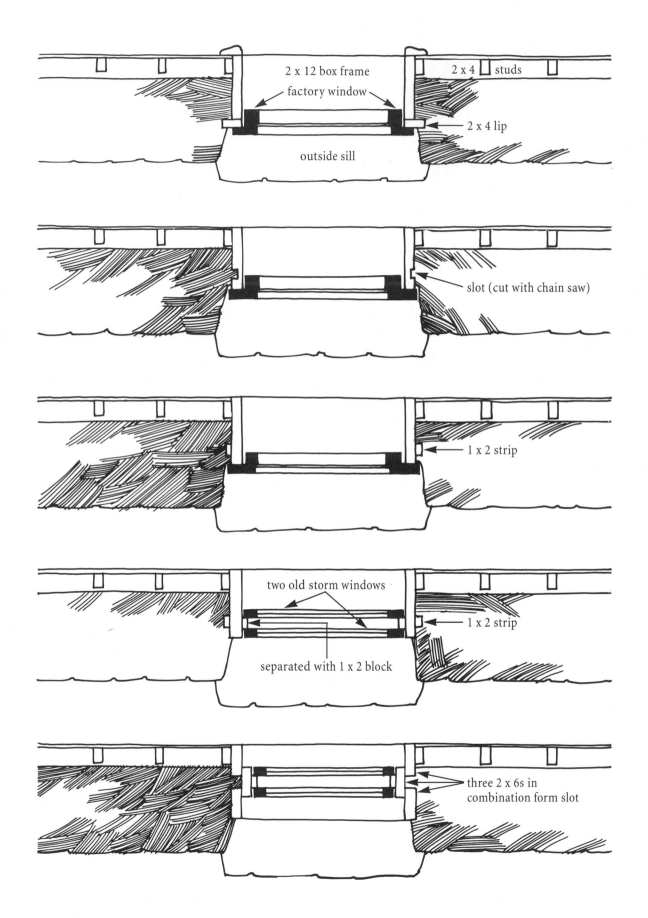

2 x 12 box frame

2 x 4 ☐ studs

factory window

2 x 4 lip

outside sill

slot (cut with chain saw)

1 x 2 strip

two old storm windows

1 x 2 strip

separated with 1 x 2 block

three 2 x 6s in combination form slot

You can assemble the window and door boxes on a flat surface and then slide them into the framed openings.

the rough opening called for will be fractionally larger than the "frame size" of the window. The window is not meant to fit tightly into the hole. The seal will be formed by the outer flange, not by the sides of the frame. The narrow gap between the window frame and the rough opening is first fitted with a few wooden wedges, or shims, to hold the window in place, and then the rest of the gap can be stuffed with insulation. (A small bundle of cedar shingles, or shakes, is invaluable as a source of tapered shims.) A tight fit between window and frame will put too much stress on the window as the building expands and contracts with the weather.

The window, however, is installed at the end of the job. Right now, the objective is to provide a rough opening of a proper size and shape to accept the window when the time does come. Apart from careful measurements, there are three important basics to remember:

1. The rough frame will be in contact with the masonry. It must, therefore, be protected against dampness and rotting. Use a preservative. Where possible, separate the frame from the masonry with sill gasket.

2. Most new lumber is green. As it dries, it will shrink and possibly warp. By the time you are ready to fit the

windows, a frame of green lumber will no longer be the same size and shape it was when you built it. This is the place to use old well-stored lumber or the more expensive kiln-dried stuff.

3. Lumber and masonry expand and contract at different rates. Any joint between the two materials will open and close as the weather changes, no matter how well built it is. And nature is just perverse enough to fix things so that the cracks get wider as the weather gets colder. The solution is to build the rough opening with a "key" so that there is no joint that runs straight through the wall without interruption.

There are any number of ways to key these openings. My favorite is to build a simple four-sided box of 2-by-12s. The inside measurements correspond to the rough opening called for in the window specifications. The outside measurements are the same as the hole left in the wall framing. (Remember from the last section that we kept the opening between the studs 3 inches wider than the rough opening called for. Those 3 inches are taken up by the thickness of the lumber in this box.)

Diagonal braces are nailed across the corners of the box to keep it square. Then the box is slipped into the opening left in the stud wall and nailed securely. The edge of the box inside the house can be lined up flush with the studs, or it can stick out ½ inch to end up flush with the surface of the plasterboard paneling. The out-

The final course of stone is brought up to a ledge on which the rafter plate will rest. Anchor bolts are set between stones to hold the plate.

side edge of the box projects well beyond the frame—into the middle of the space where the masonry will rise. When the box is nailed in place, I take the chain saw and score a deep groove all around the outside of the box. The cut is about ¾ inch deep and at least 1 inch wide. It is made only an inch or two from the outer edge of the box to ensure that it will end up well within the masonry. When the stones are finally laid around the box, the masonry will project into the groove. As the inevitable crack between wood and mortar opens, most of the key stays within the slot and keeps the wind from whistling through.

The alternative is to make a wooden key that fits into a masonry slot. This can be as simple as nailing a strip of scrap lumber around the outside of the box, instead of cutting a groove. We have also used 2-by-4s nailed to the outer rim of the box as a "lip," and we have built complex boxes of overlapping 2-by-6s in place of the 2-by-12 box. All of these methods left the requisite key and slot, but the more complicated they got, the more joints were left to caulk and eventually open up again. Two-by-twelve lumber is expensive, but it simplifies the

building of the box, and it makes a more weatherproof joint in the masonry.

That is a basic approach to framing any opening. For doors or improvised windows, it is necessary only to add a jamb or some sort of an inner lip. Figure IV-4 illustrates several options for weatherproof keys.

THE TOP PART

Regardless of how high the walls will rise, some thought must be given to the question of how the frame wall will join the roof. In a traditional stone building, this is not a serious concern. The stone walls are built, then the roof, and the inner walls are added (if at all) as an afterthought. An ordinary frame structure is equally straightforward. The rafters are seated on the top plate of the frame, and the exterior walls are stuck on later.

In this hybrid technique, though, the usual sequence is shuffled. The frame goes up first, then the outer walls, and the roof is added last. The rafters must not only meet the ridge and match one another (to avoid the wavy-roof syndrome), but they must also rest on the stone wall and still meet the top of the frame at some preordained point in space.

In theory, this is not a problem. It is easy enough to draw these three elements in a precise future fit, and as long as one follows the plan, each rafter ought to meet

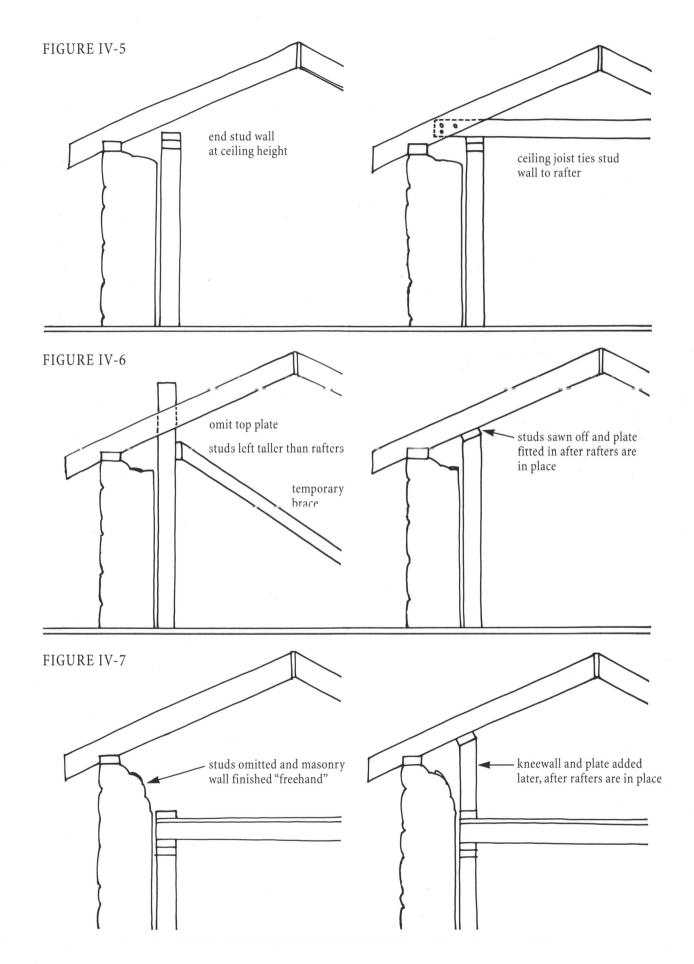

FIGURE IV-5

end stud wall
at ceiling height

ceiling joist ties stud
wall to rafter

FIGURE IV-6

omit top plate

studs left taller than rafters

temporary
brace

studs sawn off and plate
fitted in after rafters are
in place

FIGURE IV-7

studs omitted and masonry
wall finished "freehand"

kneewall and plate added
later, after rafters are in place

The ends of each stone course are tucked behind the rafter, which is raised before stone is laid in the peak.

the stone, the ridge and the frame exactly like its fellows. In theory. But then, in theory, the kids' marbles should not always roll to the same end of the room. After all, everything was level on the plan. As an amateur builder, I begin with a basic assumption that the result will never be quite as precise as the plan. I can be reasonably sure that a straight rafter will be able to meet two points in space, the outer wall and the ridge, but I know ahead of time that the third point (the juncture with the frame) is going to have to fend for itself—no matter how carefully I draw the plan.

There are at least three ways to approach the top part, each of which allows the novice some flexibility for ensuring that all the parts can be persuaded to fit.

Figure IV-5 shows the wall framed up to ceiling height. The rafter ends up somewhere above it. And the junction is made by the ceiling joist, which is nailed to the top plate, then extends beyond the frame and is nailed to the side of the rafter.

Figure IV-6 illustrates a wall of studs that was left without a top plate. It was held in place with a temporary brace until the stone wall was finished and the rafters were up (the rafters passing between the tops of

the studs). Only then were the studs marked, sawn off 1½ inches from the underside of the rafters and fitted with a top plate as a final step.

Figure IV-7 is a workable alternative for low walls. We used this approach on the upper part of the 1½-story building. The last, upper section of frame is omitted and the stonework completed "freehand," without a frame backing. After the rafters are in place, the top plate is nailed to the underside of the rafters and the "kneewall" studs are fitted in.

Regardless of which approach is taken to framing, the rafter plate, the part that bears the weight, must be securely rooted in the top course of stone. Like the sills, it stays in contact with the masonry, so it should be specially treated for rot resistance and protected with a strip of sill gasket between wood and masonry. Anchor bolts are mortared right into the wall with the final course of stone. We have found it convenient to plan the top of the wall so that the last course is all of stones about 3 inches thick. That way, the L-shaped end of a full-size anchor can be hooked under a stone, the shaft can pass up through a mortar joint, and enough of the threaded top is left sticking up to take a final leveling bed of mortar and a 2-by-6 rafter plate. Let the masonry harden for at least a day before leveling and bolting down the plates. Otherwise, tightening the nut might uproot the bolt.

One final suggestion on the subject of plates: Make sure they extend at least 2 inches beyond the corners of the building. The part that sticks out will be needed to support the last set of rafters, which will be *outside* the stonework in the gable end.

GABLES AND EAVES

With the rafter plates bolted down, the side walls are finished. The gable ends, however, are still open. In the usual scheme of things, the ridge board, rafters and roof are erected as soon as the rafter plates are ready to support them. Then the gables (the pointy bits) are filled in last. The stone house proceeds in much the same way.

We raised the studs in the gable end just as we did the side walls, except that the tops of the studs were free—there was no top plate. The first rafters raised were nailed to the edge of the studs as well as to the rafter plates and the ridge board. Thus, these first rafters secured the tops of the studs in much the same way that a top plate would have done. Those studs that rose higher than the roofline were sawn off flush.

When all the other rafters were in place, we put a final set on the *outside* of the gable end. These rested on the ends of the plates, which had been left projecting beyond the corners. The inside face of this final pair of rafters would touch the outside face of the stonework. The stone wall would rise *between* the rafters, and the last set of rafters would make a neat finish for the top

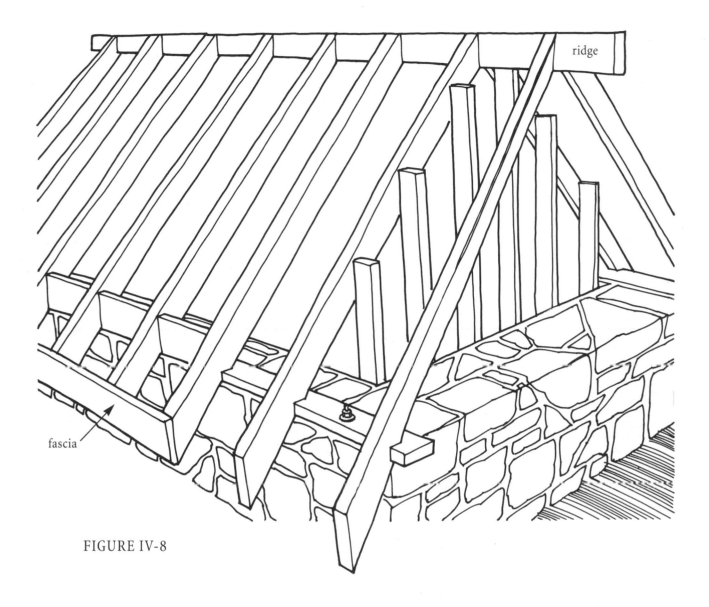

FIGURE IV-8

of the masonry, tucked in behind the rafter.

The last rafter, of course, is not necessarily the end of the roof. An overhang provides additional shelter. We let the roof boards project 24 inches beyond the gable end and added a "false" rafter at the edge. It was false only in the sense that it did not have a wall under it for support.

There are many possible ways to finish the eaves. We chose to nail short boards between the rafters at the plate, caulk around these fillers from the inside and nail a fascia across the ends of the rafters, leaving them open underneath (Figure IV-8). You could just as easily add a soffit, omit the fascia or put gargoyles at the eaves. One solution I would not recommend, however, is using stone to fill the gaps between the rafters. The plate and rafters will rot soon enough as it is. The less masonry they touch, the longer they will last.

Hand tools are enough for most amateur masons, though
a third hand and a pair of wings might be useful at times.

V Tools & Supplies

Man is a tool-using animal.

Without tools he is nothing,

with tools he is all.

—Thomas Carlyle

LUCKILY, STONE MASONRY has not achieved the level of mass popularity that afflicts the amateur woodworker. Consequently, stone tools do not come in designer colors with battery-operated attachments to stir paint and shine your shoes. The best are simple, plain and sturdily made. The only moving part is the one on the end of your arm.

One result is that the tools outlast most casual users, and quality secondhand implements are readily available at auctions and garage sales. New or used, here is what to look for.

TROWELS—These come in a wide range of shapes and sizes for special jobs. Two will be enough to build a house. You will need a large (8 to 10 inches long) triangular trowel for scooping up quantities of mortar, slopping it on the wall, working and spreading it into a proper bed. A smaller trowel, with a 3- or 4-inch triangular blade, will be useful for working in smaller spaces, pointing and finishing. Occasionally, we have used a flat finishing trowel (the rectangular one with the handle on the top), but it wasn't necessary. Start with the two mainstays, and save the others until you really need them.

There are cheap trowels on the market that won't spread butter without bending and breaking. Look at the point where the handle joins the blade. That is where most of the stress will be, and that is where the cheapies will break. The thicker and heavier the metal there, the longer the tool will last.

CHISEL—A fieldstone house has little use for a chisel. If you are going to take the time to cut more than a few special stones, then chisels are not what you need as much as an extra year to finish the job. The time does come, however, when a few stones must be cut. You will need an all-steel chisel with an extra-wide blade. A 3½-inch blade is about right. Narrow blades can be just as effective but are harder to keep in a straight line when the chisel is bouncing all over the face of the rock. These broad chisels are usually sold for cutting bricks, so ask for a brick chisel if you can't find what you want. Don't worry about a rounded blade on a used one. A few minutes on the grinder will restore the cutting edge.

MALLET—For hitting the chisel. Also for hitting the stone if you aren't that fussy about where it breaks. Don't use your good nail hammer, though—you'll break more hammers than stones. Get a 2½-pound steel mallet (sometimes called a club hammer). It looks like a miniature sledgehammer with a short handle.

MASON'S HAMMER—Few tools are more useful to the stonebuilder. It has a dual-purpose business end, with a square-faced hammer on one side and a 1-inch chisel on the other. It is ideal for quickly trimming off bumps and corners, tapping stones into place and all sorts of minor pounding and breaking. I use the handle butt almost as much as the steel end (it is less likely to shatter the stone), so look for a solid hardwood handle. The chisel end will need regular grinding to keep its edge. Philistines may refer to these as "brick hammers," but after a few days of trimming and tapping, you'll know what they are really for.

SLEDGEHAMMER—An 8- or 10-pound sledge is an optional refinement for splitting boulders too tough to be impressed with the chisel. It may also come in handy for driving wedges when splitting off slabs of bedrock or quarrying rock from ledges. More on quarrying later, but if you don't have to do it, you probably won't need a sledgehammer this big.

LEVEL—The longer the better. I know the little glass tube with the bubble in it doesn't get much bigger as the levels get longer and more expensive, but a stone wall is very bumpy, and you will appreciate the longer level's ability to average out the little bumps and indicate whether the wall, in general, is level and plumb. Make sure the bubbles go both ways for vertical and horizontal use. Plastic loses snob points but gains on washability.

STRING—A 100-foot roll of mason's line (or chalk line) is indispensable. It is the string that guides the placement of rocks and keeps the wall straight. Nylon lines are less susceptible to rot and breakage, but the natural materials hold a knot better and keep their tension.

MEASURING TAPE—A retractable steel tape is in constant use, not only for the usual construction measurements but in the regular sizing up of every stone to be fitted into the face. Don't spend a lot of money on a good one, since it will soon be jammed with cement. An old-fashioned wooden measuring stick is even cheaper and never jams with cement.

WIRE BRUSHES—Have at least two: a big one for cleaning the moss and dirt off stones before you use them, and a narrow one for brushing out cracks and crevices on the wall. Use them with vigor, and wear them out. They aren't that expensive to replace, and the alternative is a weaker wall.

CROWBARS—These are essential for quarrying and useful for shifting big building stones onto the wall. We use two: a common 3-foot wrecking bar (looks like a cane) and a heavier 5-foot straight bar when things get serious. Crowbars are really no more than sturdy levers with a flat end (for getting into cracks) and a built-in fulcrum. We have used buggy axles and saplings to the same effect.

WHEELBARROW—The heavy-duty construction, or contractor's, barrow is worth the extra cost when you are moving a couple of hundred tons of stone around the site. Look for a solid steel pan with high sides (useful for mixing small batches of mortar by hand). The undercarriage must be sturdy. Get the largest wheel available if you have any rough ground to traverse. Finally, lay the barrow on its side, and see how easily it can be tipped upright again without interference from the handles or undercarriage and without skidding away. I will explain why in the next chapter, but believe me, it matters.

SCOOP—You will need something to measure out rough quantities of sand and cement for the mixing operation. Some builders use a shovel, but I could never shovel cement from a bag without spilling the powder in all directions. We adopted a smaller scoop that was meant for taking ashes out of the fireplace. Size is not critical, since the proportions are what matter in mixing, not the absolute quantities.

MORTAR PAN—Something the size and shape of a large dishpan is ideal: large enough to catch the mortar as it is dumped from the mixer and small enough to carry when full. It helps if the corners are rounded. Then the trowel will scrape out the last dollops of mortar more easily. Metal is better than plastic for durability but harder to find in the junk (it won't be good for anything else when you are finished). The best pan we ever had was an enameled steel baby bath salvaged from the dump. A wheelbarrow will suffice for carrying mortar around the lower reaches, but sooner or later, you will need something you can carry up the ladder and balance on the wall.

PAILS—The more the merrier. Keep one at the mixer and one with the mason. Any trowels or cement tools not in actual use can be dropped in a water pail so as to be slick and clean when required. A pail or sprinkling can will be needed on hot sunny days to keep the stones damp. Five-gallon containers are handy and usually available free.

FEED SACKS—Feed sacks? Yes. Or, if you don't live near animals with a grain habit, dig out some old blankets or worn-out seat covers. A wet burlap bag, however, is the best tool we have ever found for cleaning caked cement off tools or anything else at the end of the working day. Damp bags spread over fresh masonry will keep it from drying out too quickly, and dry bags will insulate wet mortar from damaging overnight frosts.

TARPAULINS—Sturdy plastic or traditional canvas tarps are useful for protection against unexpected rain or cold temperatures.

SAWS—If you have a hand-held circular saw, it can be fitted with an abrasive disc (called a masonry, or concrete, blade). This will be useful for cutting or scoring particularly finicky jobs—thin flooring stones, for example. Heavier jobs call for a more powerful concrete saw, obtainable from tool-rental firms. We once lowered

Simple but sturdy, the stonebuilder's tools are readily available at building-supply centers or auctions.

the cellar floor 5 inches by sawing the bedrock into blocks and splitting them off with wedges. The big saws are brutishly unpleasant instruments, though, and I would not recommend them except as a last resort.

ESOTERICA—Professional masons might include an array of more specialized tools: stone breakers, bull points and a range of chisels. These, however, are not as readily available as those described above, nor are they really necessary for most amateur projects.

YOU—Your most valuable tools are those you were born with. Spare no effort to protect them. Steel-toed boots are a great comfort when moving heavy stones. Protect your eyes when cutting or hammering stone, and resist any temptation to work bare-handed in mortar. No matter how tough and calloused a worker's hands might be, the lime in mortar will dry the skin and sear cracks through to the meat. By all means, eschew the gloves if you can keep your hands out of the mortar or the stuff washed off, but some of us never quite got over the mud-pie thing, and we need gloves to be able to dabble without bleeding from the fingertips. Building-supply places sell heavy rubber gloves that last well and provide all the protection you need. I always found them

too stiff, though. I missed the dexterity and sense of touch that bare hands allow. One suitable compromise is the thin rubber gloves commonly found in the supermarket. They are made for the dishpan, not cement, so they don't last long. But you can still feel what you are doing, and they are cheap enough to replace regularly. Avoid the pink ones if you are sensitive to remarks.

THE CEMENT MIXER

The first summer that Liz and I mixed mortar in earnest, we laid a scrap of plywood on the ground and nailed on three boards as sides. We stirred the brew with hoe and shovel and somehow managed to get through the job, but our aching backs made it clear that life would be a whole lot easier with a mechanical mixer. The hoe-and-shovel mortar was first-rate—better mortar, in fact, than we have ever been able to make with a mixer. The failing was entirely ours for neglecting to stay forever young. So we went shopping for help.

The rude awakening came when the salesman warned us that the relatively cheap little numbers, so common in the catalogs, were useless for making mortar. They made fine concrete, he said, but relied on the larger aggregates tumbling around in the drum to get the job done. A simple mortar of sand, cement and water was said to require a mortar mixer. "What is the difference?"

The 5-foot crowbar can pry up stone from ledges.

you might well ask. Well, you might not need to ask, but I did. The most important difference, as it turned out, was about $2,000—$350 for a cement mixer but more than $2,000 for the mortar mixer. The cheapies had mixing blades fixed to the inside of a *rotating drum*. The mortar mixers had blades that rotated *inside* the stationary drum, scraping the sticky stuff off the sides.

Being an unrepentant cynic where commerce is concerned, I asked what would happen if I ignored the $2,000 advice and tried to make mortar in a cement mixer. "Nothing," said the salesman. "It would mix the dry ingredients, but as soon as you added water, the whole mess would stick to the bottom of the drum." Feeling skeptical and in need of the $2,000, I paid him $350 for the proletarian model and went home to see for myself. We shoveled in some sand and cement, mixed them up to a uniform gray and began to pour in the water. Sure enough, the whole mess stuck to the bottom of the drum like whipped cream in the eggnog cup. But if you tip the cup up high enough, even the last of the eggnog comes out—all over the end of your nose, but it does come. So we figured the mixer just might not be tipped at enough of an angle.

Set on the level, the common garden cement mixer spins around with the drum tipped at about a 45-degree angle, halfway between sitting on its bottom and lying on its side. With the original mess still in the drum and the drum still turning, we continued to exaggerate the angle until the drum was tipped at only about 20 degrees from the horizontal. At that point, the sticky mass flopped down from the top of the arc and folded over on itself—and continued to do so until the result was a well-mixed batch of genuine mortar. We propped the mixer up permanently at that angle, and it has made beautiful mortar ever since.

The only drawback to such unorthodoxy is that the mixer cannot work at full capacity. Since it is lying on its side, a full load would spill out of the open end. We use a 3-cubic-foot mixer and never make more than 1 cubic foot at a time—usually less. Since that is all that I can carry and all that I can use at once without the last of the batch drying out, the extra mortar is in no way missed. The $2,000 would have been missed a great deal more. By all means, get the proper machine if you can afford it, but don't give up on the economy model without a trial.

While we're still on the subject of tools, remember that your cement mixer will need a heavy-duty outdoor extension cord (to make it go around), a grease gun (to keep it turning) and some sort of cover to keep the motor dry. Like all the other tools, it will also need to be thoroughly washed at the end of the day. Put a bucket of water in the drum, along with a shovelful of sharp-edged gravel, then turn on the mixer and let it clean itself. A wet feed sack will clean the rim and the outside of the drum. Dump the water, and leave the drum in the dump position so that water can't collect in the bottom.

MAKING MORTAR

Liz, who bakes a mouth-watering loaf of bread, is also our resident mortar mixer. These two talents, she insists, are not unrelated. Both involve mixing ingredients to a texture that the expert recognizes as "right" by the way it looks and feels and acts in the pan. Recipes have little to do with it. Being a fussy type who likes to work to careful formulae measured out precisely, I was skeptical of her slapdash approach to the mixer. But I had to admit that she did turn out a fine batch of mortar. Nevertheless, I took over the machine from time to time to demonstrate how the discipline of standardized measures would improve the quality. An inordinate number of the demonstrations resulted in unusable slop. I admit defeat. In fact, I have even rationalized it:

If you consider that the amount of water is critical (add one more splash of water to a perfect batch, and it turns to instant quicksand) and that the sand you start with may contain different amounts of water, depending on whether it is a dry day or a wet one or whether you take it from the top of the pile or the bottom, then it stands to reason that the amount of water you must add to it has to vary from batch to batch. There really is no substitute for the intuitive approach.

The touch is something that has to be developed, though. You have to start with some sort of recipe, and the best place to begin is with the two measurable ingredients: sand and cement.

Sand, by the truckload, is fairly cheap. So you might as well buy the best. The biggest part of the bill will be the trucking charges, and it costs as much to haul useless sand as it costs to haul the best. Ask for screened masonry sand. Then examine it in the truck before it is dumped. It should be completely clean, free of stones, dirt and organic debris, and it should be "sharp." Look closely at the grains. Sharp sand will show facets and edges. Some of the particles may sparkle in the sun. Sand with fine, rounded grains—like river silt—makes a much weaker mortar. Pick up a handful, and rub it between your palms. The more abrasive it feels, the better cement it will make.

If you have a cheap source of "pit run" sand (as it comes out of the ground), by all means use it. But do remember that you will need to screen it to remove the larger particles. There is nothing more frustrating than wrestling a 200-pound stone onto a fresh bed of mortar, only to have it rock back and forth on a hidden pebble instead of settling in solidly. Actually, there was one experience more disheartening. That was the day a full-grown toad stuck his head out of the mortar just as I was about to drop the rock. We washed him off, and he was fine. I wasn't. Stick to clean sand, and keep it clean.

Cement is sold by the bag and comes in two basic types: Portland and masonry. Bigger suppliers will also carry quite a selection of limes and sealers and things that can be used with cement, but for our purposes, Portland and masonry cement are enough. The standard bag holds 1 cubic foot of cement powder (helpful if you are mixing large batches), and cement is always sold, measured and mixed by volume rather than by weight. Portland cement is heavier than masonry cement and nearly always more expensive.

Why two types? In broad terms, Portland makes a hard mortar, and masonry cement makes it sticky. When building with brick or precast blocks, there is no real reason to use Portland at all. The purpose of the mortar is simply to bind the blocks together. The uneven texture of fieldstone, however, means that the thickness of the joints between stones will vary considerably beyond the standard ½-inch mortar joint recommended for block building. The mortar, therefore, should have some strength of its own so that you can fill the wider gaps with confidence. In simplest terms, use masonry cement for binding and Portland for strength.

Trial and error finally brought us to a standard mortar mix that was made with 2 scoops of masonry cement, 1 scoop of Portland and 9 scoops of sand. Note that the overall proportion is 1:3 cement to sand, a ratio that prevails no matter what type of cement is used.

The 2:1:9 mix (masonry: Portland: sand) was our basic recipe for normal wall building. Where concrete was required, we used only Portland cement in the ratio of 1:2:4 (1 part cement, 2 parts sand and 4 parts gravel). Wherever a really sticky mess was needed, we worked out a dynamite concoction of sand, cement and slaked lime that stands up and sticks to anything like stale peanut butter. (See Chapter VII for more details on

Tipping an ordinary cement mixer up on blocks helps sticky mortar mix right to the bottom of the drum.

slaked-lime mixes.) But the workaday wall mix has stayed at a regular 2:1:9 and has never shown a crack or otherwise let us down.

As near as I can relate, Liz brews up her glop like this: Starting with a clean, dry mixer, she pulls the drum up to the mix position and starts it rolling. Nine scoops of dry sand go in first. Then 3 scoops of cement—2 of masonry and 1 of Portland—in either order. That gets mixed until it is all a uniform color. Then she starts trickling water slowly down the side of the drum. You can slosh it straight to the bottom, but washing it down the side cleans up any dry material around the lip. The trick is to add the water in small doses—especially near the end. It looks as if there isn't nearly enough. Most of the gunk goes around and around, stuck to the bottom like a great gray scab, and the water disappears around the edges. That's when I get impatient and slop in some more water, and the whole thing collapses into a gritty soup. Liz keeps trickling, and pretty soon, the scabby mess at the bottom starts to sag with the water and folds over on itself. At that point, it is beginning to mix, and the dry bits disappear into a churning mass of homogeneous gray. Now it needs only another trickle or two of

Stacking platforms are portable and provide several working levels and room for tools and stone.

water to lose its crumbly texture and stick together in smooth, buttery glops of mortar. Big chunks of it still ride the mixing vanes up the side of the drum, but they slide free near the top of the spin and flop back into the mass. That's the stuff!

If you are not sure whether the mix is right or not, take out a big trowelful and drop it on a board. Mix it and chop it around a bit, then smooth it into a loaf and slice off one side to leave a vertical "wall" of mortar about 3 inches high. If it slumps more than a tiny bit, the mix is too wet. If the loaf is cracked and crumbly-looking and won't trowel off to a damp, smooth surface, then the mix is too dry. The perfect mix will spread like butter under the trowel and keep the shape you give it.

Unfortunately, there is not much margin between a too-dry mix and a too-wet mix. That is why the last of the water should be trickled in—even when you're sure it is going to need another quart. And there's no substitute for experience for telling when it is ready. Even Liz ruined her first few batches. To use up these embarrassments, we found a hole in the drive that needed to be filled and declared that patching the drive was as worthy an objective as building a wall. Think of it as an educational expense.

One final warning on the making of mortar: The best of batches can be ruined by beating it to death too long in the mixer. When it gets to the right uniform consistency, take it out. Smoothing the sides of the mass with the trowel will help to keep it from drying out too quickly. So will a damp bag over the top of the pan. An occasional stir will keep it from setting up hard too soon. But leaving it to pound around in the mixer is not the way to keep it fresh. Even with damp shade and periodic stirring, no mortar will keep for more than a couple of hours without ill effect. If it is not all used by then, patch the drive with it and start a new batch.

After dumping a batch of mortar, Liz rinses out the drum with the hose and leaves it turned down in the dump position to drain. Otherwise, the crumbs left behind would dry out and come back to haunt you as lumps in the next batch of mortar. If she is starting another batch right away, she skips the rinse and simply throws in 9 more scoops of sand, 3 of cement . . .

Mixing mortar is more an art than a science. One to three is the basic proportion. Add the water last and slowly. All the rest is in knowing when it's done. Give it half a day of practice before surrendering to the temptation to let the factory do it for you. The commercial mortar mix (the "add water and stir" variety) is no more than a bag of sand and cement. The hardest part—adding water until it is done—is still left up to the customer.

Then there is the cost. A common brand-name mortar mix is now selling for a little under $5 a bag. Bought separately, at retail prices, the sand and cement in the mix are worth a little more than a dollar. In effect, the buyer is getting a lot of sand at cement prices. You wouldn't want to bother with a truckload of sand to patch the front steps, but if you are building anything larger than that, don't underestimate your ability to count out 3 scoops of sand and 1 of cement. That's the only part of it the commercial mixes do for you.

WHEN THE WALL GETS HIGHER

The last hunk of equipment that most builders will need is scaffolding. Working at anything higher than chest level is awkward and uncomfortable. As the wall grows, you will need something to keep you rising with it. You will also need a place to put the mortar pan, water bucket, tools and a large assortment of stones. A ladder will not do.

Rental firms have sectional steel scaffolds that are sturdy and handy. The problem is that stonework proceeds so slowly that renting equipment for the duration can be a costly solution. Buy scaffolds, or build your own.

We elected to build our scaffolds. The decision led to some problems. The conflict had to do with carpentry skills—mine. Without getting into a load of *mea culpas*, let's just say that my sturdy structures aren't portable and that the portable ones aren't very sturdy. Scaffolding had to be sturdy enough to hold me and the rocks and a lot of other junk. And it had to be portable enough to move from one part of the wall to another as the work progressed. To make it even more difficult, we recognized that the working platform would have to gradually increase in height as the wall grew from chest level to a dizzy 12 or more feet above the grass.

It had to be sturdy, portable *and* variable.

There were several crashing failures on the way, but we eventually arrived at a system of stacking platforms that gave us five working levels with two simple scrapwood structures. It worked everywhere but in the highest peak, and there was no need for portability there. We lashed together a single log tower for the peak and relied on the movable platforms for everything else.

Naturally, we started with a smaller, two-step scaffold. Standing on the lower step, with the tools on the higher level behind me, worked well up to about the 6-foot level. Then we simply turned the thing around and stood on the upper level. When the walls outgrew that arrangement, we switched to a larger platform and worked from that until the walls were 8 to 9 feet high. Then we stacked the two-step platform atop the bigger one, using first the lower step and finally the upper one. With a stepladder secured at one end of the long platform, we walked up and down the scaffold as if it were a set of stairs.

When a section of wall was finished, we pulled off the upper platform, removed the loose boards from the top of the long platform (just to make it lighter), moved the whole business along 8 feet and stacked it up again. At the very most, we had to move it twice a day, and the move was a five-minute job. The removable boards on the long platform not only made it lighter but allowed me to stand inside the structure and carry it single-handedly. The two-step platform could be rolled along by one person. Two carriers made the move easier, but one could do it alone when the other half of the team was busy.

The tower in the peak was a jerry-built affair of ironwood poles, 14 feet long and lashed together in an arrangement that derived most of its strength from leaning against the wall of stone. Its only laudable feature was that it was tall enough to finish the job.

The standard suggestion from roadside critics was that we should add a system of block and tackle to raise the stones to the top of the wall. This was considered (usually at the end of a long, hard day), but we never devised a method that would not create more fuss than it resolved. The person bringing stones in the barrow stacked them on the lower platform anyway. Raising them from there to the highest step of the top scaffold was a 4-foot lift that seemed unworthy of block and tackle. And anything rigid enough and high enough to hold the pulleys would have interfered with our muchcherished portability.

Don't adhere too rigidly to the shape and dimensions of our scaffolds. Apart from the essential diagonal bracing, the design evolved from the size of lumber available in the scrap heap rather than from any notion of what an ideal scaffold ought to be. It worked, but so might a thousand other variations.

*Abandoned quarries often leave behind heaps of waste that
can provide the makings of a fine stone wall.*

THE STONEBUILDER'S PRIMER

VI Stone

Vain we are to think that stone

is carved by man; it is the stone

that shapes the hand.

—Charles Long

THERE'S A LOT OF SNOBBERY involved with stone. Builders talk about this type being better than that type. Granite conjures up respect, marble speaks of money, slate is severe, sandstone humble, and fieldstone simple and bucolic. Geologists are even more class-conscious, assigning lineage and properties that leave one wondering whether it is really only rocks they are talking about.

For the average builder of the average wall, however, all that matters is whether the nearest stones are good enough to do the job. Who cares whether something spat from a volcano is harder or softer than something dribbled down the shield by a glacier? When you face the task of moving a couple of hundred tons of the things, a rock in the nearest fencerow is infinitely superior to a harder rock two miles away.

Of course, there are rocks that simply will not do, no matter how close by they are. Shales and some soft sandstones will literally break apart in your hands. There are engineering tests that can state precisely how much stress any rock will stand without cracking up. The problem with the scientific approach, though, is that even within the same pile, some of the rocks are hard enough and others are not. And you can't take every

stone to the lab. Our own testing was more simplistic. Any rock that seemed cracked, crumbly or otherwise unsound was tossed back on the stone heap. If it broke, it was rejected. If it bounced, it passed. And naturally, the farther we got from the building site, the more discriminating we became.

Perhaps a more reliable route to reassurance is to look around for old stone buildings in your area, especially the humble buildings. Chances are, they're made of local stone. Compare it to the stones you are considering for your own building. If the local variety has survived the years in another building, the odds are good that it will do just fine in yours.

Newer buildings and fancy old ones won't offer the same comparison. Again, it is a matter of snobbery. It isn't that the local fieldstone was in any way unsound. It simply had an image problem. Before we started to build, I made a worshipful round of all the old stone beauties in this area. It was utterly depressing. The façades of century-old stores and houses were so carefully cut and fitted that one had to look twice to be sure that it was really stone and not precast concrete blocks. I knew my lumpy old fieldstones were of the same

Buildings of beautifully cut stone are often façades. Behind the formal fronts is rough fieldstone construction.

composition—but the shapes! The precisely shaped blocks were obviously quarry stones. These mansions, like the more humble one I had planned, wore solid walls of local sandstone. My stone was apparently sound enough; but the question was, Was it good enough? Could we really hope to make a house from the rugged, weathered lumps that grew wild in the fields and woods?

The better class of buildings showed an obvious preference for quarry stone, and the implications of that choice bothered me for a very long time. I was almost convinced that fieldstone must have some secret inherent weakness—from too much inbreeding or living too long in the open. Almost. Then I took a walk one day and found myself *behind* these beautiful houses of quarried stone. Lo and behold, the backs of these pretentious petrified ladies were made of the ubiquitous fieldstone, every bit as knobbly and misshapen as mine. Only the fronts and corners were quarried. And to my untutored eye, the rough-cast backs were even more beautiful than the fronts—at least one wouldn't mistake the fieldstone backs for precast concrete blocks.

Modern builders, too, have a peculiar aversion to the humble stones beneath their feet. For some reason, contractors prefer to treat fieldstone as a hindrance. It is bulldozed aside and carted away, and then the house is built on cement blocks (which are later faced with factory imitations of fieldstone). One local building supplier proudly took me out to his yard one day to show off his latest shipment of "the good stuff." It was real sandstone, quarried 150 miles away and specially treated to look like fieldstone—the smooth faces all broken off to appear rough and knobbly. The shipping charges alone were astronomical. I was too polite to mention that there were a few billion tons of rocks just like that right under our feet. Something must have clicked, however. Within a year, that same supplier started stockpiling the local fieldstone that the excavators were carting away from the building sites.

All right. Enough of these snide asides on snobbery in the building business. The amateur builder, who suffers no shame from using free materials instead of store-bought, who trusts that God can make a rock as well as Domtar can, who doesn't know the difference between igneous and sedimentary (and doesn't care), must nevertheless look at a pile of rocks and decide which ones might make good building stones and which ones will not. For the amateur builder, I offer these four criteria for judging stones:

A good building stone
1. has at least two flat sides;
2. is near the building site;
3. can be easily moved;
4. cannot be broken easily without a hammer.

Only the last of these criteria has any bearing on the soundness of the building. All the rest are for the convenience of the builder. You can still make a wall by hauling big boulders across the country, fussing over the fit of round rocks against other round rocks or—worse still—trying to split round rocks to create flat ones. The building won't suffer, but the builder will. So feel free to break every rule except the fourth one.

WHERE TO FIND THEM

Geologists will cringe, but stone scroungers can classify their material into three broad groups: fieldstone, used stone and quarry stone.

FIELDSTONE is just that. It is scattered like flotsam through fields and wasteland—wherever the bedrock is close enough to the surface to yield up chunks. Weather and plowing churn these pieces to the surface, and farmers drag them away to dump along the fences or pile them on an otherwise useless piece of land.

In this part of the world, finding fieldstone is easy. Just look around the edges of any field that has ever been plowed, under fences and in the nearby woods. Some fields have great humps of laboriously piled stones dotted across their centers. Since a stone pile can't be

A good building stone is one with two flat sides, no matter where it comes from.

plowed, young trees grow up unmolested. Poke amongst the roots of tree lines and midfield copses. You may well discover old stone piles there.

Spring is the ideal time to look, before the weeds grow up to hide the rocks. That is when I go walking along old fence lines with a long steel bar in hand, swinging it like a cane. Its own weight drives the point into the ground with every step. "Thunk, thunk, thunk, clink!" Another stone has been discovered. Probe for the edge, pry it out of the ground with the bar, and look it over carefully. Rejects are pushed back into their burrows, the good ones piled up where we can see them when we come back later with the wheelbarrow.

It is sometimes worth the effort to probe around in even the junkiest-looking stone piles. There are two reasons why the worst stones will be on top. First, we can assume that the erstwhile farmer, facing a virgin rocky field, cleared off the biggest (and best) stones first. As the years of tidying passed, he turned up fewer and fewer stones, and these were smaller and smaller. The little ones ended up on top. Then a century or so of frost, rain, wind and roots wore away the edges until the stone pile's top layer looked like a collection of mossy

baseballs. Not too far under the surface of these apparent junk piles, we have found beautiful big square blocks, even cornerstones and arch stones.

Used stones may be harder to come by but can be well worth the search. Someone else has already selected them for their qualities, and you are likely to find a high proportion with flat sides and usable shapes. Poke around old foundations, particularly smaller barns and outbuildings, where stone supports might have been put up "dry" (without mortar). Dismantling a dry stone wall saves the task of cleaning off old cement and may yield an even better quality of stone, since a solid fit had to be achieved without the help of mortar.

Sometimes these old stone walls are not so obvious. Don't give up without a search. Any settled area in stone country can be counted on to produce at least a few early ruins. Liz's random probings along a nearby fence unearthed a small bonanza of useful blocks. There was no apparent order. They just seemed to be jumbled under the sod like any other fieldstones, except that these were in a remarkable concentration. The neighbor watched us digging away in the same spot for weeks. Finally, in the midst of other small talk, he casually nodded toward our mother lode of fieldstone. "You know, that's where the original barn was on this property," he remarked. "You'll find some good used stone in there." Clink.

Even the most humble buildings were sometimes raised on a bed of carefully chosen stones. We moved the old privy last year and discovered four prize cornerstones under it.

At times, the ground beside an old stone ruin can be as fruitful as the structure itself. Masons, amateur and professional, left a litter of rejected and excess stone as they worked. The mess was often left where it lay at the end of a job. Dirt eventually grew over the rubble, leaving little evidence except a sod-covered bank of higher ground around the building. The lower part of our existing barn is an old stone structure. We had no intention of tearing down a perfectly good wall and so went elsewhere for stones until the summer pigs arrived. The three little weaners were penned on the messy end of the barnyard—a shoulder-high pile of ancient junk that was too close to the barn to burn and too tangled with briars and vines to move. So we put a fence around it and turned the porkers loose. They happily uprooted all the rubbish and cleaned off the tangle of vegetation. By midsummer, we were down to bare ground. Nothing visible but a slight hump extending out 20 feet from the solid stone wall of the barn. The pigs kept rooting, unearthing stones as fast as we could wheel them away. By autumn, they had mined enough of the original masons' waste to fill every pothole in a 600-foot lane and enough good stones to lay up a solid wall for the woodshed, 20 feet long and 5 feet high.

Used stones, in some areas, can be found in the dry

stone walls that were piled up at the edges of fields in lieu of wooden fences. Few farmers bother with this laborious process today, but the old walls are still around. As is the case with any good stone wall, the decision to dismantle it should include some appreciation of the wall where it stands. If it still serves a purpose, even an historic or aesthetic purpose, be tempted to leave it where it stands.

Quarry stone—real quarry stone—is sawed, split or blasted out of bedrock. Mining a pit or a ledge, quarriers produce stones that are made of the same stuff as the fieldstones of the area, but man, rather than nature, is the agent. Nature's stones are rounded by the weather. Man's are sharper-edged, showing bright raw facets. Moreover, sawed or split stones can be given deliberate shapes: blocks, squares, keys and modules that fit more like bricks than the jigsaw puzzles of fieldstone building. Real quarry stone is expensive, though. Fortunately, there are ways of obtaining quarry stone without buying it at a quarry.

The most direct way is to go to the quarry for the freebies. Working quarries keep waste heaps of broken or imperfect pieces that can't be sold but which can (sometimes) be hauled away for the asking. When quarries are abandoned, so are the waste heaps. Quarry waste may not be suitable for sheathing banks or carving monuments, but it makes a deluxe stone for an ordinary wall in an ordinary house. We once stumbled on the remains of an old, old quarry, so long abandoned that it is now a forest. The waste heaps are still there, albeit sprouting full-grown trees, and they have lain in the open long enough by now that the once raw faces are weather-softened and mollified with lichens. They have the natural grace of fieldstones, yet fit together as snugly as quarry stones—a happy combination. That particular quarry is too far into the forest to use for more than the occasional cornerstone, but it is one more place to look when closer sources become depleted.

Every place where man attacks the bedrock with dynamite and heavy equipment acquires another sort of crude quarry stone as a by-product. Where roads are cut through rocky hillsides, where excavators gouge basements and ditches out of the crust, everywhere that solid rock is broken into smaller pieces becomes a potential source of quarry stone. One should always ask in places like that, but these are people who have attacked the stone as a nuisance—they are usually more than willing to accommodate anyone daft enough to haul it away for them. Pick over the rock when you won't be in the way.

When all else fails, it is still possible to do some minor quarrying on your own with hand tools. Slow—but possible. You will need several steel wedges (the kind used for splitting firewood will do just fine), a sledgehammer and a long steel bar. A well-weathered ledge is the easiest place to start.

Splitting slabs from a ledge with wedges and a sledge is less poetic than it sounds. More like hard work.

Scrape any dirt or loose material off the top surface, and carefully examine both the top and the face of the ledge. You are looking for cracks. On the top, you are looking for cracks that run parallel to the face and no more than a foot back from the edge. On the face, a good crack is one that runs parallel to the top surface and, again, not more than 12 inches from the edge.

Let's assume you find a handy crack along the top surface, parallel to the face. Put the thin edge of the wedge against the crack (even a tiny hairline crack will do), and tap it in with the sledge. If you are lucky, the crack will widen a tiny bit more and extend farther along the top. The object is to split a slab away from the face of the ledge. That is why we wanted a crack within a foot of the face—anything thicker would be too much to break away. And, for the same reason, if the crack starts to angle back into the hillside, forget it—there is too much mass to move by hand. Now insert a second wedge a few feet away from the first, still in the same crack, of course. Pound it in. The crack should again get longer and wider. With any luck, it will be wide enough to loosen the first wedge. Pound it in farther. Alternate between the wedges, driving them deeper and deeper.

At some point, the slab will break away from the face and tumble down to the base of the ledge. If it is a long slab, you may need more than two wedges. If it breaks but doesn't fall away, you may need the steel bar to pry the slab loose. Once the slab is off the face, you can break it up into smaller, more portable pieces with the sledgehammer.

Working from the face instead of the top involves exactly the same procedure. It can, however, be a more awkward position from which to swing the hammer. Clear away any dirt, or "overburden," from the top surface, find a crack on the face, and start widening it with the wedges until the slab breaks away from the top. Pry the slab away with the bar. Then restart the wedges in another part of the crack.

Finding a ledge with convenient cracks ready to split into building stones is a bit of luck that not every amateur quarrier can expect. In the real world, the cracks often run the wrong way. Or—equally disheartening—there are no natural cracks to exploit. That is no problem in a commercial quarry. There, they would prefer to split off big, solid blocks along lines of their own making, rather than the more erratic shapes that nature chooses. But starting your own cracks is a lot more difficult. Not long ago, small quarries used two-man star drills, later replaced by pneumatic drills, to bore a series of holes in a line along the top of a ledge. Wedges were started in the holes and driven in with hammers until the block split away from the ledge. You can still buy smaller star drills and quarry your ledge by hand, but it is a tough, slow way to produce stone.

On two occasions, Liz and I have "quarried" bedrock. In our case, the object was to make larger holes in the ground, but the by-product was a pile of usable building stone. The process is much more laborious than grunting fieldstones out of the dirt, but it does work—even with hand tools and city muscles.

We scraped the dirt away until we found "steps" in the surface of the rock. There were no obvious cracks, but we assumed that the grain of the rock would allow it to split along a horizontal plane. Placing a wedge at the bottom of a step, we drove it in with the sledge. Lo and behold, a crack appeared. We put another wedge farther along the same crack and opened it even more. Eventually, the slab broke off about 18 inches back from the edge. At times, the wedges were nearly all the way into the crack, and still the slab refused to break. A sharp blow with the hammer a few feet back from the edge would usually break off the raised section of slab. At the break, there was a new step. We repeated the process there and broke off another slab. When the top surface was moved back to where we wanted it, we retreated past the initial step and found another step even lower than the first one. A wedge at the bottom, some vigorous hammering, a little help with the pry bar, more slabs, a

Old farmsteads sometimes yield useful stones from fencerows, fallen walls and overgrown foundations.

larger hole. It took two of us a long hard day to remove no more than about 15 cubic feet of stone. Try it if you must, but don't count on producing sufficient stone to build a house. After that first exhausting day of gouging out the global crust with sledges and wedges, we crawled out of the slightly larger hole and collapsed under the apple tree with an ale. The best that Liz could manage was a feeble: "Did the earth move for you too, dear?" It did, but not very much.

CUTTING STONE

If you can't make do with what nature provides, breaking large stones into smaller ones is a feasible way to produce usable material. It is certainly easier than trying to break usable pieces out of ledges or bedrock with hand tools.

Part of the artistry of stone is the mason's skill in striking a rock with his hammer and making it break where he wants it to. For amateurs like me, cutting a stone is a matter of chance. Sometimes it works, and sometimes it doesn't. The tools are basic: a hammer and a chisel. My favorites are a 2½-pound short-handled

Cutting stone is a matter of patience, not power. Persistent chiseling along a line will crack the stone where desired.

hammer and a masonry chisel with a 31/2-inch cutting edge. The most important step is the first one—a careful examination of the stone.

Inspect the stone for hairline cracks. Usually, cracks will run along the "grain." If you are uncertain about which way the grain goes, break up some scrap stone and watch where it splits. In sandstone and limestone, you can sometimes see a pattern of parallel lines where layers of silt formed the stone.

If the stone is already cracked, chances are, it will break there first, no matter where you hit it. If the crack is where you want the cut to be, fine. Just chisel along the crack. Otherwise, discard the whole stone.

With a sound stone, try—if possible—to plan the cut *along* the grain. The technique is virtually the same as going across the grain, but the rate of success will be better if you parallel the grain. When you have decided where the cut should be, mark it with the chisel. Be sure to mark the back of the stone, too, where you want the cut to come through.

Now start chiseling along the dotted lines. Don't hit it too hard, and don't keep hitting in one place. Move back and forth along the mark with a steady, rhythmic

tapping. Too much force in one spot may break the stone prematurely and probably in the wrong place. For the same reasons, be sure the stone is resting in soft soil or sand. Anything hard underneath will concentrate the force of the blows on one spot and break it too soon.

As you chisel along the line, the mark will get steadily deeper. Eventually, a narrow crack will appear. If the crack is in the right place, pound away—it will break in the crack. Often the stone will break away along part of the intended cut and leave behind some excess. That becomes a new cut. Mark it, score it, and gradually add concentrated stress along the line until a new crack forms and opens.

We don't often go to all that bother for an ordinary wall stone. In an arch or a corner, it might be worth the effort. Most of the time, though, if the common field-stone won't fit in the place intended for it, I smack it with the hammer (the small mason's hammer) in the place where I would like to see it break. Sometimes I can make it fit, and sometimes I make gravel. The rate of success improved as I learned to use the *edges* of the hammer instead of the face, lining up the chisel edge (or the square edge of the face) with the line of the intended break. The blow is then concentrated along a straight line instead of being spread over the much wider area of the hammer's face. It is the difference between a slap and a karate chop.

One other version of stonecraft involves the splitting of boulders with a sledge. The idea is to strike a rock so that it breaks cleanly along the grain, leaving two halves with fresh, flat faces. The edges can then be trimmed off squarely for fit. This approach seems to be particularly common in stone veneers, where the flat face is exposed. Personally, I prefer to do less cutting, keeping any flat faces in the wall for a closer fit and letting the lumpy sides show.

Modern commercial quarries use saws to slice up blocks in regular shapes. These monsters are beyond the reach of individual amateurs. There is a way, however, that the amateur can saw a special stone to a precision shape. It is not the sort of thing you would want to do with every stone in the wall, but when the need arises, it is there.

"It" is called a "concrete saw" and can be rented by the day from most tool-rental shops. It uses a circular blade that looks like a thinnish grinding wheel, and it operates much like the hand-held circular saws popular with basement carpenters. The big concrete saws are usually driven with a gasoline engine, however. Buy a dust mask and earplugs to use during the operation and a bottle of liniment for the aftereffects. For cutting smaller stones, you can buy a masonry blade to fit your electric saw. The major difference is power. The ordinary electric circular saw is simply not equipped with the power to grind away at stones all day.

Close fitting of a fieldstone wall takes patience and an artistic eye—or a chisel to shape more regular forms.

Large stones are easily moved by loading the barrow on its side, then tipping it upright.

Regardless of how much power is behind it, the cut is made with repeated passes, gradually lowering the blade. And the blade shrinks quickly as the stone wears away the abrasive edge. Once a groove is sawn all around a block, a hammer blow or wedges driven into the groove will finish the job with a clean break in the proper place.

If you are blessed with time and patience, it is even possible to saw stones by hand. We once picked up some polished marble slabs from a scrap pile. The surfaces were beautiful, but the edges were broken off crookedly—much too jagged for the use we had in mind. I clamped a board across a slab to mark the intended cut and to guide the blade along a straight line. Then I took a broken piece of masonry blade and drew it slowly along the side of the board. It scored the marble surface cleanly. Sliding it back and forth along the board, with an easy two-handed sawing motion, I gradually deepened the scratch into a rut. It took more than an hour, but eventually, the hand-held blade sawed cleanly through a 1-inch slab of solid marble. That is not the kind of pace that would build a wall, but when special needs arise, it can be done.

From fieldstones as nature made them to the preci-sion cutting of polished marble, a range of stone is spanned that goes from the humble to the sublime. Every stone shares one common quality with its kin, however: Every one is heavy.

MOVING THE BIG ONES

The only tools needed are a pry bar and a wheelbarrow. The 5-foot steel bar will lift a stone out of the dirt or out of the most tangled rock heap. Once the rock is free, it can be rolled out to the wheelbarrow. If it can't be rolled, it is too big to get onto the wall anyway.

Getting a stone to the wheelbarrow is not a problem. The problem is getting it *into* the wheelbarrow. And here is where it pays to have a good barrow with a tough steel pan. Tip the barrow onto its side next to the stone. Then roll the stone into the pan as far as it will go. Now tip the barrow upright again. You will have to squat beside the barrow and grip the rim of the pan to raise it. You may also need a knee or a partner to keep the stone from falling out on the way up. It sounds awkward, but with a little practice, we were loading stones several times our own weight. For safety's sake, remember to keep your back straight, and do all the pushing with your legs.

Back at the building site, we were always reluctant to dump the big ones onto the ground again. Having raised the weight to wheelbarrow height already, we weren't

Rolling the big ones up ramps is easier than lifting. This 400-pounder would not have been possible without the ramp and a willing partner.

that eager to repeat the exercise later. So big stones took some planning. Where the wall was roughly the height of the barrow, we spread a bed of mortar, maneuvered the barrow right against the wall and rolled the stone out of the pan and onto its final resting place.

Above that height, a ramp became essential. We used an old 2-by-12 plank, but any *sturdy* board would do. One end rested on the top of the wall, the other on the ground. The stone was tipped onto the ramp from the barrow, then rolled or skidded up the ramp and tipped into place at the top.

As the wall got higher, the ramp got steeper. The steeper the ramp, the harder it became to move the stone. When the masonry rose above the point where we could comfortably roll a big stone up the ramp, the scaffolding came into use. The principle was the same. The same trusty ramp was used to roll the stone from the barrow up to the scaffold. Then the ramp was repositioned with the lower end on the scaffold and the other end on the wall. With ramps and scaffolds, we were still raising 300-pounders onto the wall at the 12-foot level.

Even the largest walls rise one stone at a time. A bed of
mortar, another stone, tap into alignment and repeat.

VII Laying Stone

The mason knows the stone is a monument

to the mountain, not the man.

—*Charles Long*

THE DAY DOES COME when there is nothing else to do but spread some mortar on the wall and place a stone upon it. There! You're a mason—well, an amateur mason, anyway. The first 1/20,000th of the wall is built. For some reason, that is the scary part. It is not as hard a job as moving stone, not as exacting as cutting stone, not as complicated as framing. And yet that first stone carries such a huge commitment that it is not uncommon to find would-be stonebuilders delaying the fateful day with endless preparations and prayers for rain. But telling anyone that it needn't be so is like insisting that the words "I do" are simple to say. There are times when those two words are pretty tough to get out, and there are times when sticking that very first stone in mortar becomes awesome.

So we will skip the first day, with all that emotional trepidation, and describe the second day in the life of the amateur mason (it's exactly like the first—just a little less intimidating).

The day's first task is to reset the forms and lines. The way we build, with a movable form at the back of the wall and an open face at the front, there will be one string to move and one set of forms.

The "forms" are really only there to keep the back side straight and to leave an air space between the stone and the wooden frame. The studs support them, so the forms merely have to be removable and leave an adequate space behind. It might be more appropriate, then, to call them "spacer" boards.

Our first spacers were panels cut from a single sheet of ⅝-inch chipboard. Each panel was 8 feet long and 16 inches wide. Three panels, set on edge and end to end, provided a backstop 24 feet long and 16 inches high. That was as much wall as we could build in any one day; so with three panels set up in the morning, we wouldn't have to move them again until the following morning. It is an advantage to cut the spacers so that they begin and end on a wall stud. Where the wall was framed with studs on 16-inch centers, the 8-foot spacer board evenly spanned six gaps between the studs. A shorter spacer that ended between two studs would leave an unsupported end and allow the masonry to push inward there.

Unfortunately, our first set of spacers lasted only one day. The theory was that on the second day, we would slide the spacers up between the masonry and the studs, ready for the next stretch of wall. We pushed, pried and

The laminate is set in first (TOP), then the chipboard spacer is slipped in behind it. Friction holds it in place as the masonry rises against the form. The spacer (BOTTOM) leaves a ventilation gap between masonry and frame.

THE STONEBUILDER'S PRIMER

FIGURE VII-1

made an impressive pile of chips but never did get the spacer to "slide" out from between the frame and the rock-hard wall. On the second day (you now see why I wanted to skip so lightly past day number one), we added some scrap laminate to the would-be space. This is the stuff that is glued to sinks and countertops. It is usually sold by brand name (Arborite, for example). Builders often have odd-size pieces left from custom work and are happy to get rid of the scraps at a discount. Sheet metal or any smooth, hard, flexible material could be substituted. The thin, water-repellent laminate was stuck in first. Then the chipboard panels were squeezed in behind the laminate.

On the following morning, it was easy enough to slide the chipboard up and out of the space between studs and laminate. The chipboard had not come in contact with the masonry, so it was almost as easy to take out as it had been to put in. At most, a little leverage at the bottom edge of the panel was needed to pop it out. With the chipboard out of the way, the laminate can be peeled off the back side of the masonry (with a little help from a trowel when it sticks). Scrape any dried mortar off the laminate.

Now you can reset the spacers. First the laminate, then the chipboard behind it—between the laminate and the studs. A few inches of the bottom edge, pushed into the space between the old masonry and the studs, usually fits tightly enough to keep the whole thing in place until the new masonry is built up against it. Usually. When friction doesn't work, a temporary nail or a prop will keep it from slipping until the new masonry

presses it back against the studs and holds it there.

The string, or guideline, shows the mason where the face of the stones should go. Stretch it a foot or so above the old masonry—just about where you would like the top edge of the face to be by the end of the day. And stretch it tightly. I let it sag one windy day and discovered—almost too late—that the breeze was bowing it straight out from the wall, a full 5 inches out of line. We usually keep the corners rising faster than the middle of the wall. Then the line can be strung from cornerstone to cornerstone. If the cornerstone isn't there yet, just nail a temporary "arm" on the nearest stud, extending out over the face of the wall.

The cornerstones can be set without a line by measuring directly from the corner of the frame. On an 18-inch wall, for example, we set the cornerstone in the mortar, then tapped it around with the hammer until each of its two faces was 18 inches from the corner stud. In fact, the guideline could be eliminated entirely by keeping each face a measured distance from the studs. That gets to be a nuisance, though. Spending a few minutes to set up a string in the morning saves a lot of measuring later.

With the spacers and string in place, you are nearly ready for laying stone. All that remains is to clear off the top of the old masonry with a wire brush. I know it is only one day old and could hardly have gotten dirty in that time, but it will shed crumbs of loose mortar that should be brushed away. Use the narrow brush to sweep out the crevices. If the top surface has dried out, sprinkle it lightly with water.

Laying Stone

FIGURE VII-2

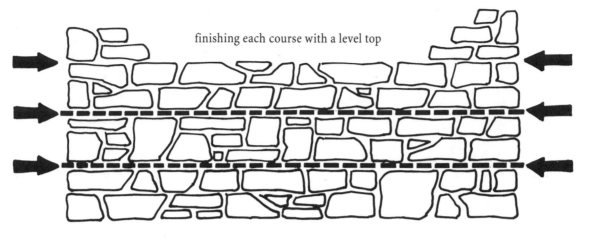

finishing each course with a level top

FIGURE VII-3

continuous vertical joint

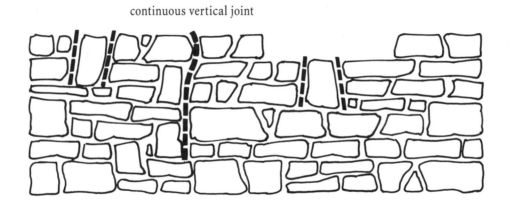

FIGURE VII-4

difficult to break vertical joints when the top is not level

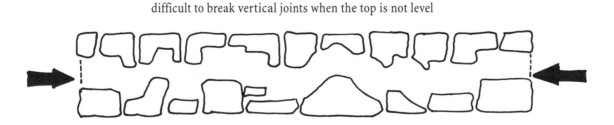

easier to accept short vertical joints within each course, then finish the
course with a level top and break the joints *between* courses

Even though stones are of very different thicknesses, the builder can stagger them aesthetically and still end up with a level top. Avoiding continuous vertical joints is critical to the strength of the finished wall.

SELECTING STONES

While the mortar is mixing, poke around the stone pile and line up the first few rocks of the day. Much of the mason's art is his ability to look at a stone and imagine how it might fit in the wall. Basically, you will be looking for these characteristics:

1. Two flat sides, or a "top" and a "bottom," if you like. A flat top and bottom provide a close fit between courses, with little or no fuss over matching shapes.

2. Groups of faces with uniform heights. Three or four stones in a row of the same height create an even top. You will appreciate such foresight when you get to the next course.

3. Faces that are long enough to bridge joints in the course beneath them. Vertical joints should be staggered.

4. An occasional stone broad enough to extend from the front of the wall to the back. Building codes refer to these as "bonding units."

Stone is best laid up in regular layers, completing one course at a time. I like to start the day with a level base and raise it by about 1 foot to a new, level top. Within that foot, there may be sections made up of several thinner layers and other areas where individual stones are 12 inches high. In other words, the heights of the faces within that 1-foot band may be staggered and staircased with stones of all different sizes, but the day's work ends with a level top again (Figure VII-2). This is not a case of petty tidiness. It really is easier to start with flat rocks on a flat base. Filling in odd holes is greatly simplified by doing it when the mortar is still soft enough to push things around a little and change the shape of the hole. The next day, when the mortar is hard, finding a rock

to fit that leftover hole gets much tougher.

Structurally, there is an even better reason for leaving a level top—even if it is only every foot or so. Bridging the joints is perhaps the most critical piece of business in the whole process of fitting stones to the wall. The object, in the official jargon, is to avoid a continuous vertical joint (Figure VII-3). Working on a level base, *any* flat-bottomed stone of the proper length will bridge joints in the course beneath it. If the lower course has an uneven top, the joints can be bridged only by finding stones whose bottoms correspond to the bumps in the lower course (Figure VII-4). That stone hunt can be time-consuming, and the builder is sorely tempted to forget the bridging and leave too many long, vertical joints. Better to level the whole wall off every foot or so, bridge every joint properly with a course of flat-bottomed stones, then fill in the spaces any old way to reach another level top.

Finding a stone with a top, a bottom and one presentable face is not that difficult in bedrock country. For the corner, though, you need a second face; and the second face should join the first one at a 90-degree angle. That is a much rarer combination. Stonebuilders horde cornerstones and would no more lavish one on a straight stretch of wall than a carpenter would use a piece of walnut as a stud. Keep a separate pile for cornerstones, and guard it (or be prepared to cut the cornerstones).

After the corners, the best stones go at the face. It looks better that way, and it is out there on the face where all the hard effects of weathering take place. Back behind the face stones, you can hide ugly rocks, misshapen ones or several little ones jammed in where no full-size stone can be made to fit.

We begin each new course at the corners, using any cornerstone that overlaps the joints beneath it. With the corners built up, we set the forms and lines and start fitting wall stones to the face. Matching heights where possible and bridging joints, we lay up several face stones before going back to fill in behind them. This order of business ensures that the least common rocks go first, where they have the fewest criteria to fulfill. With only half a dozen cornerstones in the pile, it is a relief to know that you need only find one that bridges any lower joints. From the pile of 100 wall stones with faces, you have to choose a stone for bridging joints *and* for matching heights. In the holes behind the faces, the well-fitted rock must be the right height, the right size *and* the right shape. But for that last and hardest fit, we can choose from hundreds and hundreds of odd-shaped chunks; and if we still can't find the right stone, two or three smaller ones will do. The corners, then the face, then the back.

Just as we had to bridge all those vertical joints that appeared on the face, we must also bridge any interior

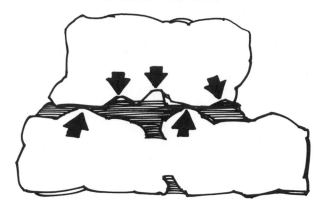

FIGURE VII-6

mortar bed not high enough
to contact all surfaces

high points prevent upper stone from settling any lower

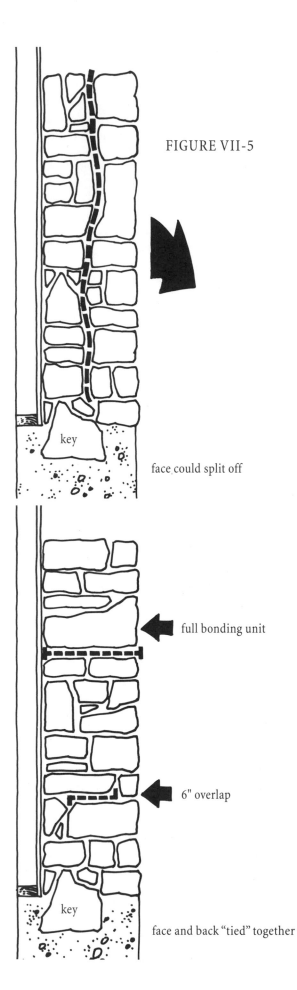

FIGURE VII-5

key

face could split off

full bonding unit

6" overlap

key

face and back "tied" together

divisions between the face and the back of the wall. In effect, we have to "tie" the front of the wall to the back of the wall. This can be as simple as putting in the occasional stone that extends all the way through the wall. In our building code, these bonding units are required to overlap by only 6 inches. In other words, not every bonding stone has to go from the face to the back. A face stone has to overlap a back stone by merely 6 inches to tie the two facets together (Figure VII-5). The code also requires that these bonding units be uniformly spaced and that they make up $\frac{1}{7}$ of the face area of the wall. So who's counting? In a thick fieldstone wall—where most of the stones are laid flat on their sides—a 6-inch overlap occurs with virtually every big slab.

We used one more "tie" in our walls. Neither logic nor the building code called for it, but it helped our neophyte sense of insecurity, so we did it anyway. At every corner and around all the openings, we built 15-foot lengths of steel cable right into the walls. Every second or third course, we laced a cable between the stones and buried it in the mortar. It is easy enough to add and (in our case) was easy to obtain—we paid $2 for a truckload of broken crane cable discarded at the junkyard. I lost interest after I saw that stone walls would stay up all by themselves, but if it makes you feel any better, by all means reinforce it.

The job of selecting stones to fit the wall is one of the most satisfying tasks of masonry. With a mental image of the space to be filled, a ruler to check the dimensions of prospective stones in the pile ("Let's see . . . we need a face about 5 inches high, and it's 8 inches to the next joint, so anything over 10 inches long would span it nicely . . . hmm.") and a hammer in hand just in case there is one that is *almost* right for the space, the mason finds himself humming as he sorts through a jumble of stones. When absolutely *nothing* will fit, there is always the hammer to take out one's frustrations on recalcitrant boulders.

With the first few stones selected and a pan of mortar at the ready, it is time to build the wall. The most finicky part of the process is the mortar. Understanding a little about how it works may help in coping with its fickle nature.

Mortar does more than fill the spaces between the stones. It is actually supposed to stick to the surface of the stones, binding them all together in a cohesive unit. The business of getting it to stick to the surfaces and cure into a hardened bond instead of a crumbly filler is behind all of the advice on how to use mortar.

The stones must first have a good surface to which the mortar can stick. A thin skim of dirt on a stone may look insignificant, but the mortar will then stick to the dirt rather than to the stone, and the stone will be free to slip out of the wall. Each morning, every stone and the top of the wall should be scrubbed clean with a wire brush.

The rituals of tapping stones into place and "chopping" the mortar onto the wall are also part of the effort to get the mortar to adhere to the stone surfaces. In both cases, the object is to work out all the little air pockets, bringing the mortar into contact with the whole surface of the stone and the wall—not just the high spots. The more of the surface that the mortar touches, the more strongly it will adhere.

The most vital thing to understand about mortar, however, is the difference between drying and curing. When water is mixed with sand and cement, the ingredients undergo a chemical reaction. When the reaction is complete, you have created a new substance. It is no longer sand and cement and water. Without that essential chemical change, the water would eventually dry out and leave nothing behind but the sand and cement—a crumbling powder instead of a permanent bond. The water is an essential part of the reaction. If the water is removed too soon (if the mortar dries before it cures), the chemical changes stop and some of the mortar is left as useless sand and cement.

It is most important, then, to keep the water in the mortar until the hardening process is complete. All the tips on wetting the stones, keeping the finished work damp, shading the work from the sun—all these are concerned with keeping the water in and keeping that chemical change going as long as possible.

Even the cautions about working in cold weather are directed at maintaining the curing reaction. If the mortar gets too cold, the curing reaction slows down and eventually stops. The comfort of the mason has nothing to do with it.

That is the theory. The practice is to scoop up a trowelful of mortar and slap it on the wall. Yes, *slap*. Drive the

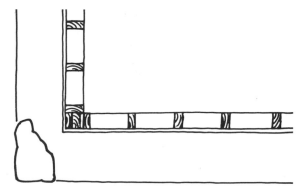

1st — cornerstone

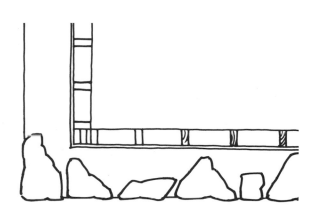

2nd — face

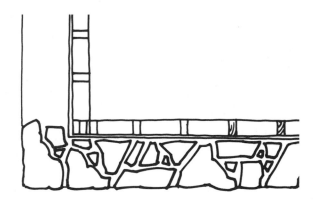

3rd — fill in behind

FIGURE VII-7

mortar into all the little nooks and crannies. Spread it over the surface, and chop it back and forth with the edge of the trowel. The necessary thickness of the mortar bed depends on the shapes of the stones. A stone with a lumpy, uneven surface will need a mortar bed thick enough to squish up into all the dimples before the high spots of rock meet and prevent the stones from coming any closer together (Figure VII-6). Stones with flat surfaces will need less mortar. Do avoid the temptation to compensate for irregular rocks by stuffing in fist-sized pockets of mortar. One consequence of too much

The mortar bed is slapped and chopped onto the wall (TOP), *filling all the spaces beneath. Stones are tapped* *or wiggled into the mortar* (BOTTOM) *until they are solidly seated in the bed.*

THE STONEBUILDER'S PRIMER

Pointing is done after the mortar stiffens. Running a wet finger along the joint will leave a smooth finish.

wet mortar in one spot is that it may slump out of place, leaving an air pocket and possibly falling right out of the wall. Better to keep a bucket of smaller stones at hand to tuck into holes.

The bed of mortar, especially a thick bed, should be kept well back from the edge of the wall. How far back depends on how evenly your stones meet. When you settle a stone onto the mortar and tap it in, some of the mortar will be squeezed out of the joint. At the back and the sides, it doesn't matter, but on the face of the wall, the mortar falls to the ground and is wasted or dribbles down the stones below and spoils their appearance. Practice will tell you how far to spread the mortar, but if mortar is falling out of your joints, it is either too wet or too near the edge.

Now grab the first stone to go on the wall. Give it a quick going-over with the wire brush, and—if necessary—wet it down. A dry stone set in wet mortar will soak up water from the mortar, drying it too quickly and ending the curing process prematurely. If the stone is too wet, however, it will turn the mortar sloppy and send it dribbling out of the joints and down the face of the wall. Fieldstone, left out on the damp ground, rained on and dewed on for a few millennia, has already absorbed a certain amount of natural moisture. So wetting depends on the weather. In hot, dry spells, I soak every stone and regularly sprinkle the top of the wall with the watering can. In damper weather, nature does it for me. The easiest way to tell for sure is to put a few rocks in the wall and see whether the mortar on them starts to dry or dribble.

Take the clean, slightly damp stone, and set it on the bed of mortar. Check the fit. Remember to keep the vertical joints staggered. Does it sit solidly in the mortar, or does it wobble on some hidden bump? Wobblers have

to be lifted off and their bumps removed. If the bump can't be removed, shim all around it with small flat stones, add more mortar and check the fit again. When it fits on the bottom, snug it up to the stone beside it, check the face to be sure it lines up neatly with the string above, and tap it gently into the mortar. Now fit another one beside it.

After several face stones are set, go back to fill in the spaces behind and between them (Figure VII-7). At the filling-in stage, work more mortar between the stones. Use the point of the trowel to push mortar in from the top, working it up and down until all the gaps are filled. The driest mortar goes into the vertical joints at the face. You should work it in well from the face and from the top, and if the mortar is the least bit too wet, it will flop out of the joints and into your boots.

At the face, you probably took some care to match the heights of the stones. Their top edges now resemble a level surface—or, at worst, a few regular steps that won't be too hard to mirror in the next higher course. The back surface is likely to be a little more rough and ready. Now is the time, when the mortar is still wet, to fill in all the odd holes and depressions with small rocks from the scrap pail. Bring it up to a level surface with stones. Don't bother leveling the top with mortar. The only mortar on top should be a fresh bed for the next full course of stones.

Now set a few more face stones, fill in behind, and level it off again. When the first joints of the day are firm enough to stand some pressure from above, you can go back and add another layer to the top. That's all there is to it. One stone at a time builds the wall.

Except on the hottest, driest days, the mortar joints on the face are totally ignored for hours at a time. Smoothing and fussing them up to look "right" while the mortar is still fresh will do more harm than good.

At the end of the day (or sooner if the sun is beating down), go back over all the new joints, pushing the mortar firmly back into the crevices with trowel or fingers. Where there are gaps, pack in more mortar, but make sure it is on the dry side. When all the cracks are tightly filled, wet a finger and smooth out all the joints. The mortar should be fresh enough to smooth out easily and firm enough to stand up in the joint without flopping out.

There are fancier forms of pointing: troweling the joints to bring them out flush with the rock surface or "roping" them to stand out like welts. But, for the beginner, raking a new joint smooth with a fingertip gives a professional-looking finish with a technique that 5-year-olds find easy.

In some spots, a smoother finish is needed. The top surface of a windowsill, for example, is just not the place for the rugged indentations of a finger-tooled joint. When a smooth surface is needed, leave the rough joint

FIGURE VII-8

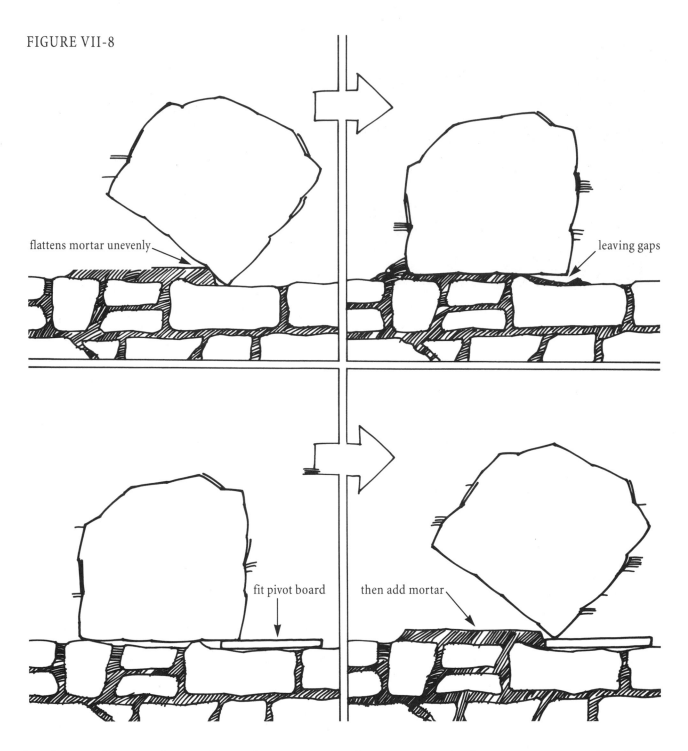

alone for several hours to firm up, then push new mortar in on top of it, smoothing it off with a wet trowel. The pointing mix will stick better if it is richer in lime. Use masonry cement instead of Portland, or add more cement in proportion to the sand (1¼:3 instead of the usual 1:3).

For a pointing mix that will stick to anything, try adding a slaked-lime putty to the mortar. You will need a bag of hydrated lime and a 5-gallon pail. Fill the pail half full of water, and stir in the lime until it is the consistency of heavy cream. Leave it to brew for a day or so, then stir it up again. Now mix a lean batch of mortar

(2 scoops of Portland cement to 9 scoops of sand). When it is just a tad on the dry side of done, throw in a full scoop of the wet lime goop and finish the mixing. Counting the lime, the cement-to-sand ratio is now the usual 1:3. The mortar, however, sticks like glue—just try cleaning it off your scoop. It also dries to a bright white finish, so don't expect it to blend in with adjacent gray cement joints. Incidentally, this lime/Portland/sand mixture of 1:2:9 makes a superb compound for plastering the chinks in a log building.

EXTRA-HEAVY STONES: Every once in a while, the mason is struck with a foolhardy urge to plunk a behe-

A small board under the back of the stone acts as a pivot, allowing the stone to drop squarely onto the mortar.

moth block onto the wall. Large blocks do take up more space than the little ones and use less mortar and make the job go faster; but I should also admit that there's a little bit of ego involved too:

"How on earth did you get *that* monster up there?!"

"Well . . . ahem . . . it was nothing really."

We treated the movement of biggies in the last chapter. There are also a few different techniques for mortar-ing them into the wall. The biggest problem is getting the giants onto the mortar bed without squishing all the mortar out of one side. The secret is to use a slightly stiffer mix than usual, keep the mortar bed well back from the face and set the rock *squarely* onto the mortar. The weight will still flatten the mortar, but as long as it flattens evenly, it doesn't really matter.

When a block is too heavy to lift and has to be rolled into place, it has a tendency to flatten the mortar on one side as it tips (Figure VII-8). Get the block into place first—before the mortar is spread. Then find a gap around the bottom, somewhere at the back or side. Slip

A course of stone is laid in sequence: first the face, then the back and—finally—rubble and mortar in the gaps.

a board or a flat stone into the gap—not far in, just enough under the edge of the big block to hold it when you tip. Now tip the block back on the board, and balance it there while someone trusting spreads a bed of mortar under it. When you ease the stone down into place again, the back edge (or pivot point) is raised off the wall by the thickness of the board. With any luck, the block will come down squarely on the mortar and squish it out equally on all sides.

FOUL-WEATHER TIPS: Fresh masonry is a creature of moderation. Too much of just about anything is bad for it. Rain washes mortar out of the joints; wind and sun dry it out too quickly; cold temperatures affect the curing. The best you can do is try to protect the masonry against minor assaults of the climate until the cure has run its course.

A sudden shower is the most frequent problem and almost the easiest to counter. Fasten a tarp over the work in progress, and take the rest of the day off. That wasn't hard, was it? Don't worry about the previous day's work. It should be hard enough to shed a shower with impunity. In fact, if it weren't raining, you would be wetting down the wall with a gentle hosing anyway—

just to keep it from drying out before it is cured.

The drying effects of wind and sun should be offset by covering freshly finished mortar with a tarp, feed sacks or anything that will shade the mortar and hold some of the moisture in. When the surface hardens, wet it down several times a day for three or four days. Finally, remember that water evaporates from a rough surface more quickly than it does from a smooth surface. The mortar on the wall or in your pan will stay fresher longer if you keep the exposed surfaces smoothed with a trowel.

The cold is the hardest enemy to fight. Building codes say the masonry and mortar must be kept at 40 degrees F or more for at least 48 hours. However, an overnight frost is not quite the disaster it would appear to be. In the first place, the masonry stores heat during the day and cools off much more slowly than the air around it. Secondly, as the mortar cures, it generates some heat of its own accord. The heat is a by-product of the chemical reaction going on between the cement and the water. If you can trap the stored heat and the chemical heat, mild frosts can be beaten off without resorting to portable heaters. We use the ubiquitous feed sacks on the wall as insulation and cover the whole thing over with a well-weighted sheet of plastic. If there are not enough feed bags to go around, loose straw or even some hastily raked leaves will add enough insulated air space under the plastic to trap the heat in the wall overnight.

FINISHING AT THE ROOF: Finishing the eaves was discussed in Chapter IV. After the roof is on, however, there remains the job of filling in the gable ends, or "pointy bits," as Liz insists on calling them.

Acrophobia and/or exhaustion can afflict the stonebuilder here and tempt one to finish the gable ends in wood or some such thing. Sheer momentum carried me up into the peaks, and frankly, it just looks so damned good that Liz has almost forgiven me for that outburst of madness.

The rafters are supported at the eaves, and so the stone in the gable bears none of that weight. It serves no other function than to fill the hole. Consequently, it is possible to make the wall slimmer as it rises here. Possible, but we had windows, arches and vents to incorporate and so kept to the same thickness until we got to the last few courses. Even there, I felt it would be imprudent to reduce the walls to less than 12 inches thick.

The chapter on framing suggested that the last set of rafters ought to fit right along the outer face of the masonry. As the wall rises into the peak, the last few stones at the end of every course are tucked neatly in behind the rafter. A little mortar between the rafter and the stones seals the junction against squirrels and storms.

Right up in the apex, where you can no longer reach in behind the rafter, the final few courses will have to be

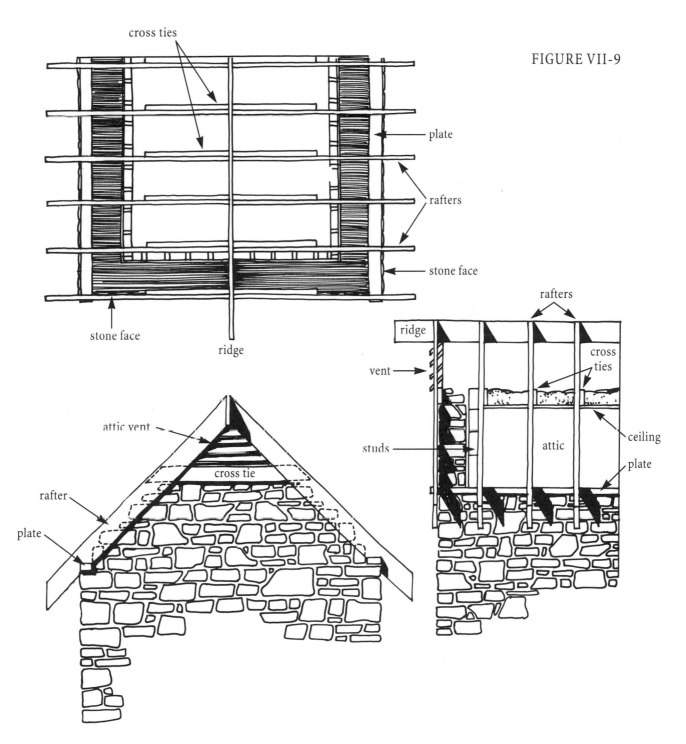

FIGURE VII-9

laid from the inside—actually working from the attic and going back outside only to finish the pointing.

An easier alternative is to leave an attic vent in the apex and carry the stonework only as high as the cross tie/rafter tie/ceiling joist. The cross tie is nailed *inside* the last set of rafters so that the outer face of the stone wall is still inside the rafter itself but rises directly *underneath* the cross tie. An extra course of masonry behind the cross tie seals the junction. This allows the builder to do all the masonry from the outside, reaching in through the triangular hole at the top to lay the final course behind the cross tie. With the stonework done, we nailed in some 1-by-3s for louvers, stapled insect screening to the inside and called it an attic vent.

Arch stones, unlike birds, can't defy the pull of gravity. The "me first" urge to fall keeps them jammed in place.

VIII Arches

An arch never sleeps.

—*Hindustani proverb*

EVEN STONE BUILDINGS need doors and windows. And when every opening replaces tons of stone that would otherwise have to be hauled and heaved into place, builders like me—who tire easily—plan on lots of gaps. The openings, however, must be spanned at the top. Here is where the stonebuilder tests his mettle.

Several options are available. If you are happy with the hybrid look, switch to something lighter—like wood—over windows and doors. Or lower the roofline, and let the eaves cap the openings. But if you are a true addict, if you really love stone, if you glow when you stand back with mortar-caked hands and admire your wall, you will have visions of stone floating over those voids. It's the icing on the cake. It's the look-Ma-no-hands touch that tempers your labor with love.

In theory, the easiest way to continue a stone wall over an opening would be with a lintel—one solid piece across the gap. The problem with that approach, however, is finding a suitable stone. It must be solid, sound (no incipient cracks) and long enough to leave at least 6 inches resting on the wall at either end. Though it may be possible to find fieldstone lintels for very narrow openings, normal windows and doors would likely need

a custom-cut stone and a small crane to put it in place.

You could eliminate the stone hunt and the crane by pouring a concrete lintel on the spot. You could—but then you could save yourself even more work by using those glue-on stones that come in 4-by-8 sheets.

Alternatively, you could treat the wall as if it were veneer and span the gap with a steel lintel. Professional masons do this all the time. The stone wall continues across the flat part of the steel angle just as if there were no opening beneath it. The only problem is that it *looks* like veneer.

Unless you can find a real stone lintel, the only way to make a stone wall look like a real stone wall is with a real stone arch. Believe it or not, it is not that hard. It just takes careful fitting and a lot of faith.

Building a stone wall is more a matter of perspiration than of skill. That is why we amateurs love it. Gravity and a good foundation keep it up. The arch, however, appears to defy the laws of gravity, and that is where faith comes in. You just have to *believe* that all those tons of masonry can stay up there all by themselves—with nothing under them but air or glass or a flimsy bit of window frame. Even if you do understand the physics

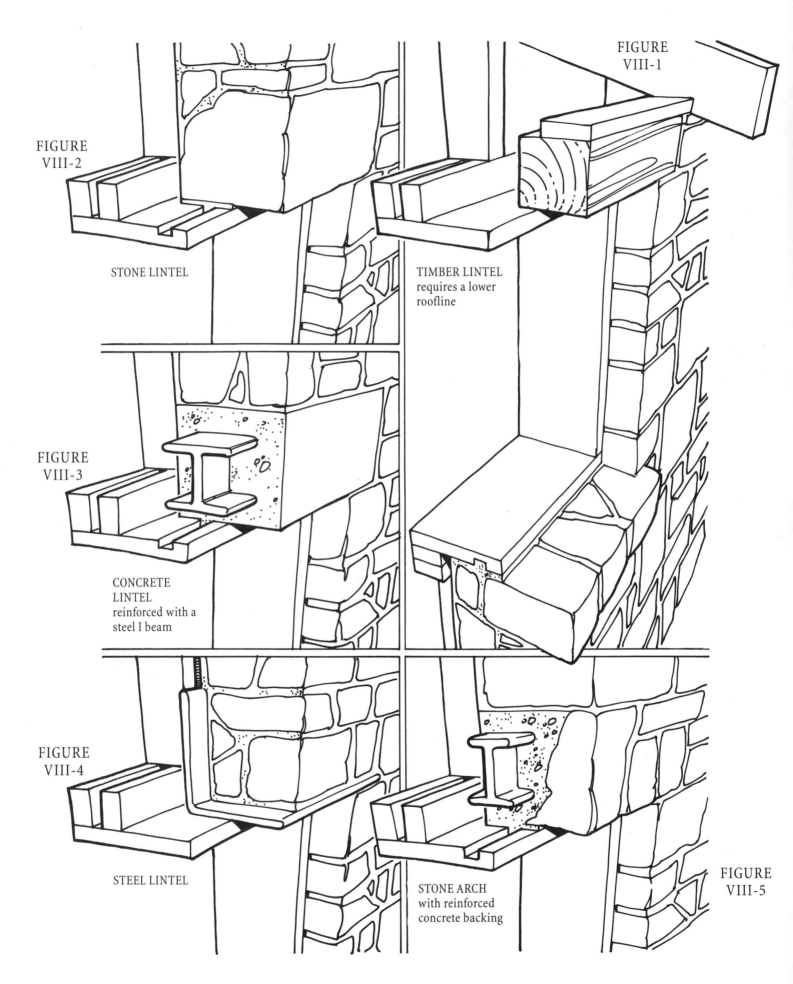

FIGURE
VIII-1

FIGURE
VIII-2

STONE LINTEL

TIMBER LINTEL
requires a lower
roofline

FIGURE
VIII-3

CONCRETE
LINTEL
reinforced with a
steel I beam

FIGURE
VIII-4

STEEL LINTEL

STONE ARCH
with reinforced
concrete backing

FIGURE
VIII-5

THE STONEBUILDER'S PRIMER

The opening is boxed with a rough frame (LEFT), then the sill and the sides are built around it. RIGHT, a traditional arch in a fieldstone wall.

of it, it's hard not to cross your fingers and avoid black cats on the day you pull out the props.

If faith alone is not enough, consider that the force of gravity—far from being defied—actually helps to keep the arch suspended in space. An arch consists of a number of stones set on edge and slanted toward the center of the opening. The center stone, called the keystone, is wedge-shaped—wider at the top than at the bottom. Together, these stones are wider than the opening beneath them. They all want to fall through simultaneously. Together, they can't. They're too wide. So the downward force becomes a sideways force. In effect, each stone tries to push its neighbors aside so that it can fall down first: the "me first" theory of gravity. It is the sideways pushing that gives the arch its strength. As long as there is ample support at the ends of the arch (remember that sideways push is transferred right into the wall) and as long as no stone is narrower at the top than at the bottom (otherwise, it might be pushed down and out of the pack) and as long as you keep the faith, the arch will stay up, like a crowd trying to jam through a doorway.

Just for fun, my 6-year-old and I stacked up a free-standing fieldstone arch one day. No mortar, just rough, uncut fieldstone piled up from the ground. She was amazed that it stayed up by itself. I felt it was futile but tried, nevertheless, to explain why it worked. "Well," she said, "if they would just cooperate and take turns, they could all fall down." Fortunately, neither stone nor gravity is as clever as children.

PREPARATION

It is considerably easier to lay masonry against wood than to fit wood to the bumps and curves of fieldstone. In other words, if the opening is to be framed for a window or door, start with the framing, not with the stone. Whether you use salvage, prefab or custom-made windows and doors, they all have to be placed in some sort of wooden frame. The frame is built first, then the masonry is built up around it. After the opening is capped with a lintel or an arch, and preferably after the roof is on, the window or door can be fastened into the opening formed by the wooden frame.

Every builder has his own favorite method of framing openings, but in a stone building, there are three additional considerations:

• First, the joint between masonry and wood should not be allowed to extend straight through the wall but should be interrupted with a slot and "key." Chapter IV

Steel lintels have a modern look (TOP LEFT). Wooden lintels (TOP RIGHT) look more traditional but are subject to *wood rot. Fieldstone arches (BOTTOM RIGHT) or cut stone arches (BOTTOM LEFT) are permanent and beautiful.*

A good arch stone must have flat, almost parallel sides for the tightest, strongest fit.

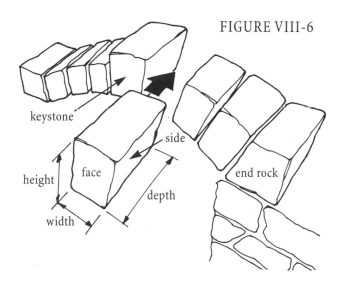

FIGURE VIII-6

keystone

side

height

face

depth

width

end rock

THE ROCK HUNT

The hardest part of building an arch is finding the stones. On the face of it, they should resemble parallelograms or slightly lopsided rectangles. The height should be greater than the width. The sides should be fairly flat to fit closely against adjoining stones. And ideally, the depth would extend through the full thickness of the wall (Figure VIII-6). Don't despair, though. Nature doesn't make a perfect arch stone. We have to help out a little, and even then, the results are rarely ideal. As long as the three basics are satisfied (wider at the top, solid ends and plenty of faith), you should not be stricken with fallen arches.

Most of our building stone comes from fencerows and fields—stacked up there with the broken plow points. They are old and mellow, with weathered faces and round, mossy corners. They make a beautiful wall. For arches, we go elsewhere. Into the woods, under the leaves, at the back of a ledge or under an aging stone pile—where weather and plowing have not had a chance to round them. Straight edges and flat sides replace aesthetics as prime criteria. You might not look so far afield for a supply of ordinary building stone, but you can bring home the makings of an extraordinary arch in the back of a pickup.

My favorite source is a long, low ledge, a barely perceptible 12-inch outcropping that snakes and bumps through a half-grown woods. You wouldn't break stride for it ordinarily. But pull back the leaf mold, and look more closely. There's a clutter of broken rock in front of the ledge itself, broken off by time, weather and roots. Most are half-buried. The top of the ledge shows cracks where time will eventually produce more small stones from big ones. The cracks follow the grain of the rock: clean, straight, parallel lines. The pieces that break off along these cracks have flat, parallel sides—the basic requirement for an arch stone.

With the long steel bar, I pry aside the weathered

illustrates several ways to key these openings.

• Secondly, in most cases, the rough frame can be used as part of the temporary support for the arch. It can even be used as part of the form for a concrete-backed arch. In any case, be sure that the frame is strong enough to hold the weight of stone or *wet* concrete (wet concrete is much heavier than dry is). Once it is set, the arch will hold itself, so don't feel you have to frame with railroad ties. However, in that critical wet period, a lighter frame may have to be braced temporarily with 2-by-4s.

• Finally, the rough frame will be in permanent contact with the masonry and should be treated against rotting and, if possible, protected with sill gasket.

With the rough frame in place, the sill is mortared in under it. The sill is there to shed water, so select some smooth-topped stones, set them on a slight angle, let them stick out at least an inch beyond the face of the wall, and finish the top joints with flush pointing. The stones up the sides of the opening are set in just like any other stones in the wall. The only extra care the mason takes is to keep the stones outside the space needed for the window's outer flanges (the "overall" dimension; see Chapter IV).

The flat arch (LEFT) *has begun to crack. A rounded arch* (RIGHT) *is stronger but requires wedge-shaped stones and a fanlight to fill the gap.*

clutter on top and look for buried stones. After digging out a collection of possibles, I sort them all by size. Structurally, it matters only that the height of the face is greater than its width, but stones of a uniform height make a prettier and more practical job. Uneven heights would complicate the laying of the next course above the arch.

The collection of possibles is then lined up in a long dry run at an arch. Right there in the woods; there is no reason to carry out all the rejects. Set on edge, just the way they would go in the wall, they usually lean to one side or the other. Depending on which way they lean, they're designated "righties" or "lefties" and placed in a group to the appropriate side of the imaginary keystone. Now is the time to check the fit within each group. They are shuffled and reshuffled to get the sides as closely matched as possible. The less mortar that has to go between them, the better. Don't worry if the depth of a stone is too great. You can always knock off the back end with a sledge. The sides do have to be closely matched, however. If the underside will be exposed— over a doorway, for instance, or a deeply set window—

you may want that to be fairly flat as well.

When the stones are as good as nature could manage to make them, go over each one with a chisel to knock off bumps and corners that spoil the fit. Now set them up on edge again, and try rearranging the order. They may fit more closely in one sequence than in another. Set up a group of stones, push them together, then measure the total length across all the faces in the group. Then try another arrangement, and measure that. The shortest grouping is the tightest fit.

At this point, consider the final appearance. Maybe I was toilet-trained too early, but I like the neatness of symmetry in an arch. It looks stronger even if it isn't. So I try to arrange the righties in a mirror image of the lefties. Suit yourself on appearance, but don't sacrifice a tight fit for a neat façade.

When you are satisfied with the two groups of arch stones, remember the order, or mark them with chalk, and haul them back to the work site. I know it sounds unreasonable, but bring back a few of the rejects too. Just in case.

THE SETUP

With the stones at the job site, the worst is over. From this point on, it is more artistry than muscle. With that in mind, stand back for a good long look, and decide

FIGURE VIII-7

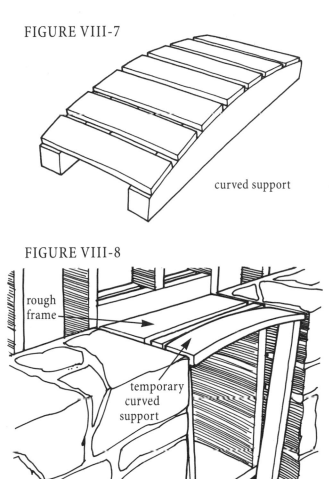

curved support

FIGURE VIII-8

rough
frame

temporary
curved
support

props

A warped board provides temporary support and sets the curve for the arch. Once the stones are selected, do a test fit on the support.

how much curve your arches should have aesthetically. The choice is only partly technical. First make sure it is going to look right.

Technically, the flatter the arch, the weaker it is. But even a flat arch is possible. In fact, it is fairly common in the traditional Scottish stone masonry around these parts. It is not often used on wider spans, though, and cracks seem to develop after a century or so. At the other extreme is the semicircular, or rounded, arch. It is stronger but requires that your stones be wedge-shaped. It also means installing a fanlight or similar filler for the gap between the arch and a flat-topped door or window. Personally, I prefer a slight curve. Just enough curve to strengthen the arch but not enough to require a fanlight.

How much curve? I've traced elliptical sections, transferred curves from other plans, even tried it free-hand. Nothing worked quite as well as going behind the

barn and rummaging in the scrap heap for the most badly warped board I could find. The warp determined the curve, and that board is a key piece in all my arch constructions now.

If you are a tidy builder with no warped boards about, you will have to make a curved support to hold all the stones above the opening until the arch is complete. The curve at the top of the support determines the curve of the arch. Trace the curve on two pieces of scrap 2-by-6 (you may need wider planks or even plywood if your arch is more rounded), and then nail shorter boards across the curve (Figure VIII-7).

To avoid building a new support for each arch, make the first one long enough to fit the largest span. When the biggest arch is done, pull out the support, saw enough off each end to fit the second largest span and proceed. This also ensures that the curve of each arch is identical. It is the sensible way. However, we of limited faith like to start practicing with the small arches first.

Anyway, cut the support to fit the gap—not too tightly, though. Remember that you have to get it out again when the arch is finished.

Now, using 2-by-4s or anything else that will serve as "legs," prop up the curved support at the top of the opening. The props can rest on the sill, the ground or whatever is handy. Just make them long enough to hold the top of the support at the point where you want the bottom of the arch to be. And again, if you must use nails, remember that you will have to dismantle it from *underneath* after the arch is set.

If the inner part of the arch is to be supported on the rough frame, the curved support should be wide enough to fill the rest of the gap (Figure VIII-8). Regardless of how the arch is supported, a neatly finished support is pointless. My warped board takes the weight and—roughly—sets the curve. The bumps, cracks, knots and wiggles are insignificant compared with the irregularities of the stone. Nor is it necessary to curve the permanent framing or match it closely to the bottom of the arch. If the ends of the curved support line up with the corners of the permanent window framing (the rough framing), then the curved support will be higher in the middle. In the center of a 4-foot span, my precious warped board is 3 inches higher than the flat-topped window frame—hardly enough to worry about. The arch stones follow the higher curve, and the narrow crescent beneath is easily filled with mortar or concrete.

With the supports in place, it is time for a trial placement of the stones. Set them up on the curved support. Three or four inches of the last arch stone should rest solidly on the wall itself. In other words, these last stones will sit partly on the curved support and partly on the wall. Wiggle the stones, rearrange them, and shim them up with stone or wood chips until you find a solid fit.

We now have two sides of an arch, and the most important piece is missing. I have left the keystone until last simply because it is harder to find. The ledge I use for arch stones splits naturally along parallel planes. A wedge shape, which we need for the keystone, would occur only with an erratic grain or a break angling across the grain on one side. Nature doesn't often do it that way, so I usually have to make the keystone the hard way, with hammer and chisel. As long as I have to cut one, I might as well leave it until last and custom-cut it to fit the gap. There is one consolation: The keystone can be higher than the arch stones, so the search-and-sort mission is simpler by one criterion. Look for a stone that matches the angle of the adjoining arch stones on one side and that is also at least as high as the arch stones. Then it is only necessary to make one cut to match the other side of the arch.

When it is cut, fit the keystone and center it in the gap. Snug up the other pieces until they are tight all the way across. With a piece of chalk, mark the wall at each end of the arch. Now you are ready to lay up wall stones to meet the ends of the arch at the chalk marks.

The object is to lay a course of wall stones to the same

The end rock is mortared, ready to take the first arch stone.

height as the top of the arch stones. This is the buttress that will carry the lateral force, so treat it with almost as much care as you would the arch itself. You will need a flat, slanted side on each end rock (to match the slant of the last arch stone). This is where those rejects from the pile of possible arch stones come in handy. Leave an inch or so to spare between the end rock and the arch. The arch stones never seem to go back in as easily with mortar as they did on the trial run. I once made the mistake of building the wall right up to the chalk marks, then had to recut the keystone to make it all fit again.

LAYING THE ARCH

When the wall has had a few hours to set (the end rock should not be able to move in the mortar), you are ready to tackle the arch itself. Faith or not, this is a tense time. You will want to work quickly and carefully. It should be laid up in one short session so that after all the stones are in, the mortar will still be fresh enough to let you tap any of the stones back into alignment, pull out the errant ones for trimming, shim them into better symmetry and fiddle about until it is straight and solid.

Mix up a good, stiff batch of mortar. Too sloppy, and it may run out of the bottom of the arch.

Start at one end by troweling a layer of mortar on top of the wall and up the slanting side of the end rock already in place. Set the first arch stone into this bed of mortar, and tap it home. Remember that you have only an inch or so of tolerance, so bring it up tightly. Now

The keystone (LEFT) is dropped in last, from the top. Mortar is worked into the joints from every side (RIGHT), filling all possible gaps.

spread more mortar on the bare side of the first arch stone. Set up the second stone, and tap it in. When you've finished one side, start the same way at the other end. The keystone goes in last. Spread mortar up the sides of the last two arch stones, and lower the keystone in from above. If it takes a few light taps of the hammer to bring the keystone down to the curved support, congratulate yourself on a perfect fit. If it is too tight, try to push the arch stones closer together. Otherwise, you'll have to do some fast trimming with the chisel. If it is too loose, distribute the gap evenly and work in some more mortar.

Now quickly align the stones. Any bowing in or out from the straight line of the wall must be corrected immediately. Shimming and tapping should settle them into neat order. When it is as straight as you can make it, use the trowel to ensure that no gaps remain in the mortar. Work it in from the front, the back and the top of the joint.

Pointing the face of the arch is no different from pointing any other part of the wall. The underside of the arch, however, is inaccessible until the curved support is removed. Wherever you can, slide the trowel along the

bottom of the arch—between the stones and the support. Be careful, though, not to dislodge any shims. The object is to separate the mortar from the temporary support. You can't really hope to give it a proper finish; you will still have to come back to complete the pointing later. But slipping in the trowel at this stage will make it easier to remove the support later.

Voilà! You have an arch. If you want a feeling of exhilaration, pull out the props and supports now, while the mortar is still soft. If you are lucky, the whole arch will drop a tiny bit and settle into a tighter, stronger fit. Don't try it with a long span, though—it may sag out, away from the wall as well as down. After one such scare, I've given up the dramatics and let it harden for a few days.

WHEN THE STONES FALL SHORT

Unless you are really fortunate, not all the arch stones will extend to the full thickness of the wall. You will have to fill in at the back. A sound filler here and there won't make much difference. But if there is a fair volume of space to fill, consider using concrete. If most of the stones are short of the full wall thickness, you may even want a reinforced concrete backing. It adds strength and would offend only the fussiest of purists. The arch stones do, after all, carry the full weight above them and are no less authentic for having a little help. This is how:

Pulling out the supports can be tense, especially when the mortar is still wet (as was the case here). It still comes as a surprise that all those stones can stay up by themselves, with no visible means of support. Look, Ma. No hands!

THE STONEBUILDER'S PRIMER

A concrete form is already in place. The braced window frame (the rough frame—don't try this on top of a factory-built window) or the temporary support will serve as the bottom of the form. The arch stones, already in place, will provide the front of the form; the ends of the space are closed off by the end rocks on the wall. Set a backboard against the studs, and you are ready to pour.

Do consider the timing, however. The concrete will adhere to the arch better if the mortar is still fresh. On the other hand, unless the mortar has partially set, the weight of the fresh concrete pouring in behind it could push the arch out away from the wall. A couple of hours' delay seems to provide a suitable compromise between "fresh" and "set." Use this time to push a little stiff mortar into any holes or open joints on the inside of the makeshift form.

Reinforce the concrete with a 6-inch steel I-beam. A construction-supply yard will sell them and usually cut them to length for you. Get a beam at least a foot longer than the span so that 6 inches or more will rest on the wall at each end. If you're going to use steel, remember not to build up the end rocks too close to where the steel will rest. You have to leave room for the beam and a few extra inches for wiggling it into the concrete.

Pour the concrete into the form until it is several inches deep on the bottom. Then put the steel in the form, and work it back and forth until the concrete oozes up around it. Next, fill in around the beam and over the top with more concrete. During the filling operation, keep prodding with a rod or trowel to work out the air pockets and settle the wet concrete all around the steel. When the beam is completely covered and the concrete is level with the tops of the arch stones, cover the whole thing to keep it damp, and leave it alone for a few days (Figure VIII-5).

THE MOMENT OF TRUTH

On the first fine day when you are overwhelmed with confidence or curiosity or both, gather family and friends for the great unveiling. Warn the audience to stand well back (unnecessary, but it adds to the drama), and knock out the props and supports. Pass a hand through the ether beneath those tons of stone. Climb to the top, and bounce on the keystone. "Look, Ma, no hands!"

Knocking out the props inevitably leads to some quiet thoughts on just exactly how much weight that arch will be able to support. At what point will Atlas shrug?

The mathematics required to determine the strength of an arch involves some complex engineering calculations. A general approach is futile, since the calculations depend on specific data on these particular stones' characteristics (compression strength, for example), the type

and proportions of mortar, span, curvature, distribution of the load above, and so on. Then, to calculate the "safe" limits of the arch design, the engineer must consider variables such as foundation design and soil type, how the "live load" of the interior floors is transferred to the walls, even the propensity for earthquakes. In short, it is virtually impossible to generalize about design strength. Each arch is unique. Even the building codes recognize the futility of generalizations by ignoring the load limits of masonry arches, except to refer vaguely to "proper design." Certainly the unique and varied problems of fieldstone arches are beyond the reach of standardized rules.

If the absence of scientific certainty threatens to deter you from putting arches in your homemade house, stop a moment to consider that arches have been built successfully for thousands of years, often by people who couldn't calculate anything over 10 without removing their sandals. Arches have been around much longer than the computers that predict their limits.

If you are reinforcing the arch with steel or a steel and concrete backing, you can at least draw some comforting comparisons with standard rules of building. For example, the Canadian Residential Standards do give guidelines for supporting a 4-inch stone veneer on steel lintels. A steel angle with a cross section measuring $3\frac{1}{2}$ inches by $3\frac{1}{2}$ inches by $\frac{1}{4}$ inch is permitted across a span of 7 feet 7 inches. A span of 10 feet 11 inches requires a lintel with a cross section of 6 inches by $3\frac{1}{2}$ inches by $\frac{1}{4}$ inch.

British standards (based on BS 449:1959) suggest that a 6-inch-by-$4\frac{1}{2}$-inch steel I-beam weighing 20 pounds per linear foot would safely carry an evenly distributed load of 20.2 tons over a 4-foot span, or 10.1 tons over an 8-foot span. Encasing the I-beam in concrete strengthens it considerably (refer to it as a "composite beam" if your building inspector asks).

These standards cannot, of course, be applied directly to arch building or even to arch reinforcing. They must be carefully qualified and applied only to the intended building technique before they can be used with confidence. I state them here in oversimplified form only to provide some rough idea of the strength of steel supports.

The best answer for the home arch builder, short of hiring an engineer, seems to be *overbuild*. On those occasions when we've had to add a composite beam to the back of an arch, we've been careful to far exceed whatever vaguely comparable standards we can find. Over the usual 3-to-5-foot spans, we now use 6-inch steel I-beams encased in best-quality concrete.

This may be far more strength than will ever be needed, but we don't have to flinch when the kids slam the door.

A frivolous touch carries an added impact in stone, which,
if left completely unadorned, might seem severe.

THE STONEBUILDER'S PRIMER

IX Special Touches

The beautiful rests on the foundations

of the necessary.

—*Ralph W. Emerson*

HALFWAY THROUGH AN ORDINARY WALL in an ordinary house, the amateur mason can be afflicted with some extraordinary symptoms. The first is a new respect—almost an affection—for the material. At the same time, it is easy enough to become jaded with laying one stone after another in a wall that is beginning to seem endless. Love and ennui, together, can be resolved only by turning to something a little different, something a little more exciting than another rock in the wall. Arches give the artisan some of the romantic satisfaction, as do some even more frivolous uses of stone. These touches may not make a wholly practical contribution to a "walls and roof" house, but they do put some sparkle back into the job.

STONE FLOORS

With a supply of reasonably flat stones, it is a simple job to install a flagstone floor in any room of the house that does not have an excavation beneath it. A room over a crawl space is ideal. The procedure is crude, but it works:

1. Apply foamboard insulation to the inside of the foundation wall.

2. Fill up the hole with rubble, tamped earth or sand to within a foot or two of the desired level (sand is preferred because it doesn't settle or compact).

3. Rake the surface smooth.

4. Place a layer of foamboard insulation on the surface, making sure it rests evenly on the fill with no hidden air pockets underneath.

5. Add another bed of sand.

6. Seat stones firmly in the sand.

7. Brush more sand into the joints.

If the stone floor is not to extend from one foundation wall to another—in other words, if it has to abut a normal wooden floor at some point—you will need to contain the fill with a retaining wall (Figure IX-2). The retaining wall doesn't have to be fancy. Block or stone laid up dry (without mortar) will do just fine for most low walls. The top stone of the retaining wall is also a floor stone. A minute gap left between the retaining wall and the wooden joists will allow the wooden floor to bounce in its accustomed fashion without disturbing the solidly set stones.

Setting the stones in the sand is the most painstaking part. Start by putting any square-cornered blocks in the

A retaining wall may be needed to hold the fill under a flagstone floor. This one was built dry, and mortar was added only to the top course.

corners of the room. Then fit in the other pieces like a giant jigsaw puzzle, digging sand out of the bed or adding to it, depending on the thickness of each stone. Leveling the surface is aided by the use of a board long enough to reach from one side of the floor to the other. The bottom of the board shows where the top of each stone should be. The most difficult stones to fit will be the final ones, so try to finish in an inconspicuous spot where a mosaic of smaller pieces won't be noticed.

Tightly fitted joints are much less trouble if you can trim the edges off squarely. Use the chisel, or put a masonry blade in the power saw. We laid the mudroom floor with stones as nature made them. The next floor, however, had to include a trap door and an iron grate set flush in the stones to cover the hole. Here the joints and the rim of the hole were trimmed with the help of chisel and saw. The closely fitted grate sits snugly in its place.

Once the floor is laid, the joints are best ignored for several months. Brush some sand between the stones, and put the floor to use. The fill may settle in places, upsetting the level surface, and individual stones may prove to be poorly seated, sinking on one side or wob-

bling as you walk on them. Readjust these misfits as they become apparent. When they look right—and stay that way for several months—you can commit the floor to more permanent joints. Brush the sand out of the crevices to a depth of 2 or 3 inches. Then sprinkle the cracks with water, and work in a regular mortar mix. Trowel them off flush with the surface of the rock. Keep them damp and untrodden upon for three or four days.

If the stones are properly seated, the mortar in the joints is merely cosmetic (well, it does make sweeping easier too). The mortar is not really necessary to keep the floor in place. The stone floor in our mudroom entrance was in place for more than four years before we got around to filling the joints. In that time, the mortar-less floor was sorely abused by wheelbarrows, a herd of goats and stampedes of 6-year-old hockey players with skates and sticks. Not a stone was out of place when we finally brushed out the sand and replaced it with mortar.

Apart from being unusual, attractive and indestructible, these floors are also surprisingly easy to insulate. The 2-inch foamboard can be broken between your fingers, but laid out flat on a smooth bed of sand, it is solid enough to resist compression by several feet of fill and stone. Rather than taking the cool, damp character of the earth beneath them, insulated floors stay as warm and dry as the air in the house. A baseboard and quarter-round trim will cover the top edge of foam at the wall.

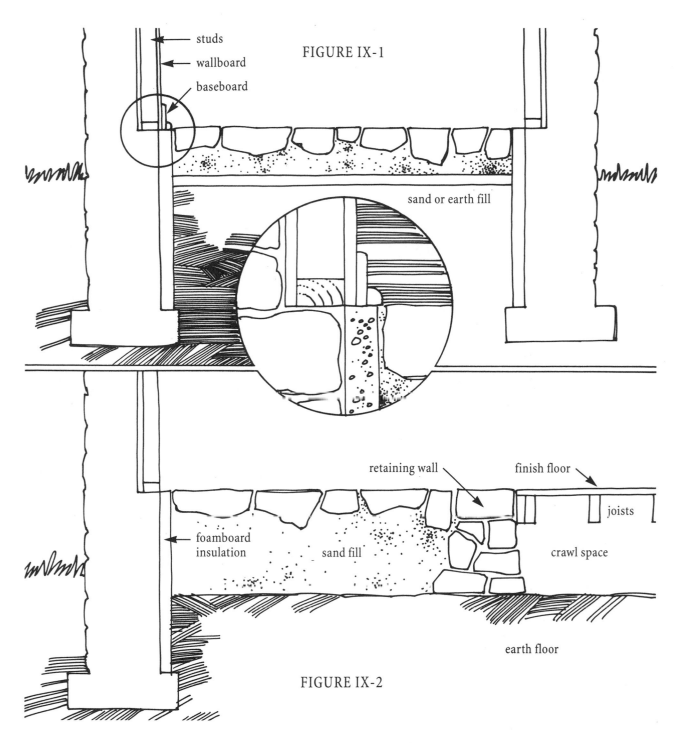

FIGURE IX-1

studs
wallboard
baseboard

sand or earth fill

retaining wall finish floor

joists

foamboard
insulation sand fill crawl space

earth floor

FIGURE IX-2

INSIDE WALLS

The people inside a homemade house of stone really have to love the stuff. Let's face the fact: Vinyl siding is a whole lot easier to lug around. So the look, the texture, the feel of stone are all important to the amateur mason—otherwise, why bother? And yet the only way you can see the stone is to go outside. The beauty of one's hard-earned nest should be available to those inside as well as to passing motorists.

In some climates, it might be feasible to expose the inner surface of a solid wall, but anywhere north of banana country, insulation is *de rigueur*. Still, we wanted to see the stones.

The compromise was the construction of an inside masonry wall. In our case, it was a small wall between the kitchen and the woodstove. It was also a support wall, bearing the weight of the upstairs floor joists. (After all, why waste the strength of stone on a mere partition?) The important consideration was to separate it from the exterior wall to prevent the conduction of precious heat from the inside to the outside.

The inside wall is built exactly like an outside wall, except that, in our case, the wall would be visible from

Flagstone floors may be insulated with foam panels; the top edge of the panel (LEFT) can be seen under the window. This stone floor (RIGHT) has a fitted trap door.

both sides, so it was built in traditional style (with two faces rather than the slipformed back). We poured a foundation right on bedrock. If bedrock had not been accessible, it would have been necessary to estimate the weight of the wall and calculate the required bearing surface for a footing (see Chapter III). Being inside the house, the footing would not have had to be placed below the frost line. We finished the concrete foundation at floor level and carried on in stone. This time, there were two sets of guidelines—one for each face.

Where the stone abutted the frame wall, we separated the masonry from the studs by temporarily placing scraps of chipboard and laminate against the studs (Figure IX-3). These worked exactly as the spacers did in ordinary wall work. When removed the following day, they left a flush, "formed" surface and a narrow space between the frame and the masonry. Later, when the time came to finish the inside walls, the space between masonry and studs was just wide enough to slip in the Gyproc panels that covered the rest of the wall. The result was a neatly finished junction between the stone and the "plaster" wall.

Like the floors, the stone wall inside the house moderates the temperature by soaking up heat for storage when the woodstove behind it is blazing away. After the fire dies, the wall keeps radiating its heat into the room.

DRY STONE WALLS

Long before we ever mixed a batch of mortar, we lived in a busy city neighborhood that seemed to be overrun with middle-size boys on bicycles. We shared a driveway with neighbors who harbored one of these angelic terrorists. Actually, he was a charming kid, but his morning routine was unshakable: slam the kitchen door, vault into the saddle, "wheelies" up the drive, a sharp left across our front lawn and full speed to school. Grass and petunias were cleft by a rut that had to be either paved or damned. We dragged home load after load of big, flat stones and stockpiled them until we had enough to stack up in a knee-high border all around the barren thoroughfare that we hoped to make a garden. The finished "structure" was the shakiest-looking piece of work that man has ever inflicted on rocks. I had doubts that it would last the night.

Bright and early, we heard the slamming of a kitchen door, 10-year-old sound effects of viciously shifted gears and the popping sound of an imaginary clutch, wheelies up the drive, a sharp left and . . . . The bike, in a some-

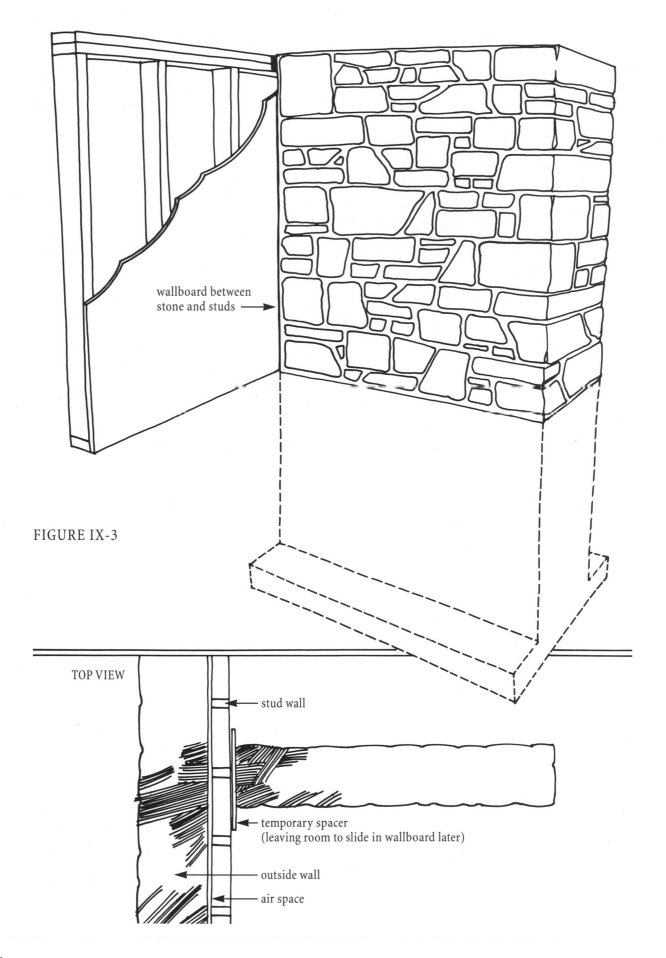

wallboard between
stone and studs

FIGURE IX-3

TOP VIEW

stud wall

temporary spacer
(leaving room to slide in wallboard later)

outside wall

air space

Dry stone walls (TOP) come apart from the top down. The heavier stones should be on top. An inside wall (BOTTOM) *should be separated from the outside to stop heat conduction. (See Figure IX-3.)*

THE STONEBUILDER'S PRIMER

FIGURE IX-4

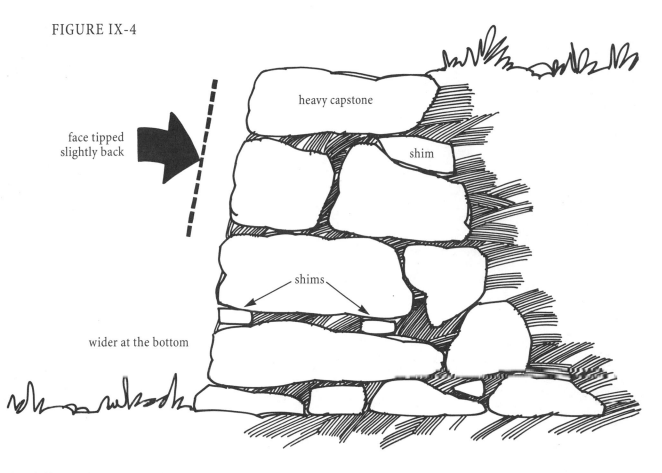

face tipped
slightly back

heavy capstone

shim

shims

wider at the bottom

what different shape, was still in the drive. The boy was in the flowerbed, dignity and petunias equally wounded. The wall—the wobbly, wiggly, patently amateur pile of stones—was completely unscathed. Now, nine years later, we drive by the old place from time to time and marvel that there is still not a rock out of place.

The dry stone walls we are building now are still simple, functional and attractive. They are also much less wobbly than was the first attempt.

There are really only two basic differences between a solid wall and a random pile of wobbly stones: careful shimming, and saving the best stones until last.

The shimming is what takes out the wobbles. It is no more complicated than collecting a bucket of thin, flat stones and jamming them under any rock that can be wobbled. Put a big stone on the wall, and try to rock it by pushing down on the top in several places. If it rocks, put a shim in the gap at the raised end. In a masonry wall, this job is largely taken care of by the mortar.

The easiest dry stone wall to build is one that is built against a bank of earth, as in a retaining wall or a terrace. The earth props up the wall as much as the wall props up the earth. Better still, a thin layer of earth between the stones does as much to prevent the wobblies as mortar does. Shovel the dirt in behind each course of stone, and tamp it down hard with your heel. Then rake some loose dirt forward, over the top of the

stones. Pick out the pebbles (they cause more wobblies than they cure). The next course of stones is wiggled into the dirt just as you would tap stones into mortar. Shim as needed (Figure IX-4).

A freestanding wall has two solid faces with rubble in the middle. Without the dirt, it takes more shimming than a retaining wall. It also takes more stone for the extra face.

In general, a shim gets shoved under any edge of a wobbly rock that shows a gap. If you have a choice, though, it is better to shim the back side of a stone than the face. Shims can work their way out of the face, but at the back, they are held in place by the dirt fill or by the rubble in a freestanding wall.

One common mistake in dry wall building is to get the thing upside down: the big stones on the bottom and the little ones on top. It is understandable. After all, the importance of solid footings is stressed in every other type of masonry. A dry stone wall, however, falls apart from the top down. The lower stones rarely come out until the stones above them fall off the wall. Without the mortar, there is nothing to keep the top intact but weight. Consequently, the heaviest stones should be up there to hold everything in place.

It is prudent to build a dry stone wall with its base a little wider than its top and to keep the faces sloped slightly back into the center, but proper footings are

Low, outside walls are often better off without the mortar. The wall will flex with minor heaving. Putting the bigger stones on top helps hold it together.

largely redundant. In most cases, it is sufficient to start by laying the first course right on the dirt. A massive wall on soft soil will undoubtedly suffer some subsidence, but with a dry stone wall, subsidence or frost movements make little difference. Without any mortar to crack, the joints can flex with the movement of the wall and recover themselves in such a forgiving fashion

that it is impossible to tell that they moved at all.

For that very reason, it seems obvious that most low-slung outdoor walls (terraces, planters, steps, border fences and bicycle barriers) are actually better off without mortar. A solid masonry wall must start below the frost line with a solid footing. Without that precaution, the joints will surely crack. The dry stone wall, on the other hand, is built from the ground up. Who cares if it sinks 2 inches? The worst that can happen is that it might spit out a shim or two. Shove them back in, tap them home with a hammer, and your (invisible) repairs are finished for another season.

NICHES AND SHELVES

The first niche I carved for myself had no more noble motive than laziness. The working day, the woodshed wall and the pile of building stones were all nearly finished. In fact, the stone pile was more nearly finished than the woodshed wall—about five stones shy of what was needed. I laid a few flat stones in the gap as a shelf and reduced the thickness of the wall above the shelf from 16 inches to 6 inches.

In that case, the niche was at the top of the wall and didn't need to be capped. It did, however, prove to be a handy place for storing tools and an easy way to eliminate the need for about 300 pounds of stone. And so we planned another niche in the workshop wall. This one had to be capped with a simple arch and in fact was treated much like a window. There was no framing, and the hole did not go all the way through the wall, but it was a hole, and it did save some lifting. Granted, it's not a simple way to build a shelf. A couple of brackets and a board would be considerably faster. But, well, all right, it was *fun*. And it was a pleasant break from putting another ordinary stone in an ordinary wall that was beginning to seem endless.

Providing for future shelves, brackets, hanging pegs and so on is a simple matter if you think of it while you are building the wall. Just insert the peg, or whatever, right into the mortar.

More commonly, you remember where the coat pegs go only *after* the wall is finished. It isn't quite as easy, but it is still possible to make the necessary holes in the masonry. You will need a variable-speed drill and a special masonry bit. In sandstone or limestone, you can drill just about anywhere. With something harder, like granite, confine yourself to drilling in the mortar joints.

Where a screw is required—with shelf brackets, for example—drill the hole and insert a masonry plug. These used to be made of lead but are now more often plastic. They are relatively cheap and are available at any hardware store. The package will stipulate the size of hole required. Drill the hole (at a slow to moderate speed), insert the plug, and turn in the screw.

Wooden pegs can be very attractive in stone. Drill a $\frac{3}{8}$-inch hole (the largest masonry bit suitable for the standard $\frac{3}{8}$ variable-speed drill), stick in the dowel with some epoxy cement, saw it off to the desired length, and hang your fireplace stocking with no fear of its falling.

If you don't have a fancy drill, you can still make the necessary holes with an old-fashioned star drill. This looks like a thin steel rod with an X-shaped point on one end, and the other end blunted for hammering. Hold the drill loosely in one hand, and tap it lightly with a mallet until the hole is started. Rotate the drill slightly with every hit of the hammer. It makes as neat a hole as the electric drill—it just takes a little longer. Insert the dowel with epoxy cement, the same as for a drilled hole.

Building with standard materials results too often in a standard house—uniform, homogenized and impersonal. The stonebuilder, however, is free to mortar in any old thing that strikes the fancy.

A particularly handsome stone can be highlighted by setting it on its end, contrasting its vertical position with the usual horizontal placement of more ordinary stones. Unusual stones can also be given a featured prominence by projecting them slightly from the face of the wall or by recessing them a little from the rest. Contrasting textures, colors and sizes can be built into the face with as much artistry as the mason cares to apply.

One nearby family, halfway through their fieldstone house, took time out to build a fireplace in the living room. Every member of the family scoured the fields for a special stone, a personal memento, and each mortared his own favorite into the face of the fireplace—just below the mantel.

Another friend, building a staircase of fieldstone, left a special place for 4-year-old Jake's handprint and "signature." A factory-built modular home just can't be that personal, or that permanent.

Fireplace plans have to consider the chimney's route to the roof and how that affects joists, windows and rafters.

THE STONEBUILDER'S PRIMER

X Fireplaces & Chimneys

Now stir the fire and close the shutters fast,

Let fall the curtains, wheel the sofa round,

…So let us welcome peaceful evening in.

—William Cowper

THE GLOWING HEARTH, once a fixture in every house, has become a place of compromises. The essential question is whether to have a fireplace at all. An open fire warms the heart as well as the toes, and Christmas wouldn't seem like Christmas without the flames of a big birch log to drive away the solstice. Sadly, most fireplaces are also notoriously inefficient heaters. Some even cause a net *loss* of heat from the house.

I wish it weren't so. Forced to choose between practical considerations and aesthetic ones, some of us just have to grit our teeth and close our eyes to efficiency. By all means, build a fireplace, but accept it as warmth for the psyche. Wood burns better in a stove.

Roland Thomlinson built our first fireplace. He was an old-fashioned craftsman who cared as much for the beauty of stone as modern contractors care for their bank accounts. He built us a prize, with heat exchanger, raised hearth, cooking crane, the works. It was the sole heat for the house and the center of family life through four Canadian winters. We loved it. We also nearly froze to death. Beauty has a price.

Compromise rears its ugly head again over the choice between the traditional solid masonry fireplace and the prefabricated fireplace form. The steel forms have an enormous advantage for the amateur mason: All the guesswork is removed from the tricky business of getting the throat in proportion, the smoke shelf properly shaped, providing for the flue exit, the damper, and so on. All those doubts are resolved in the prefabricated form. The mason merely has to cover it up with stone and add a chimney—stone on stone, just the way we built the wall. Moreover, the double-walled forms offer built-in technical advantages of their own: heat-circulation ducts for greater efficiency, outside-air intake, optional fans to boost circulation and doors. The price of all that built-in convenience is money ($400 and up) and longevity. Steel rusts, and it warps at high temperatures. Most units come with a 20-to-25-year warranty, but even the best of the steel forms won't last as long as firebricks and stone.

Masonry fireplaces endure. They won't heat up a room as well as double-walled steel, but they do endure. The offsetting risk is smoke. The essence of a fireplace is the proportions of its innards. If the chambers and passages aren't shaped just so, the smoke wafts into the room rather than up the chimney. In a book intended

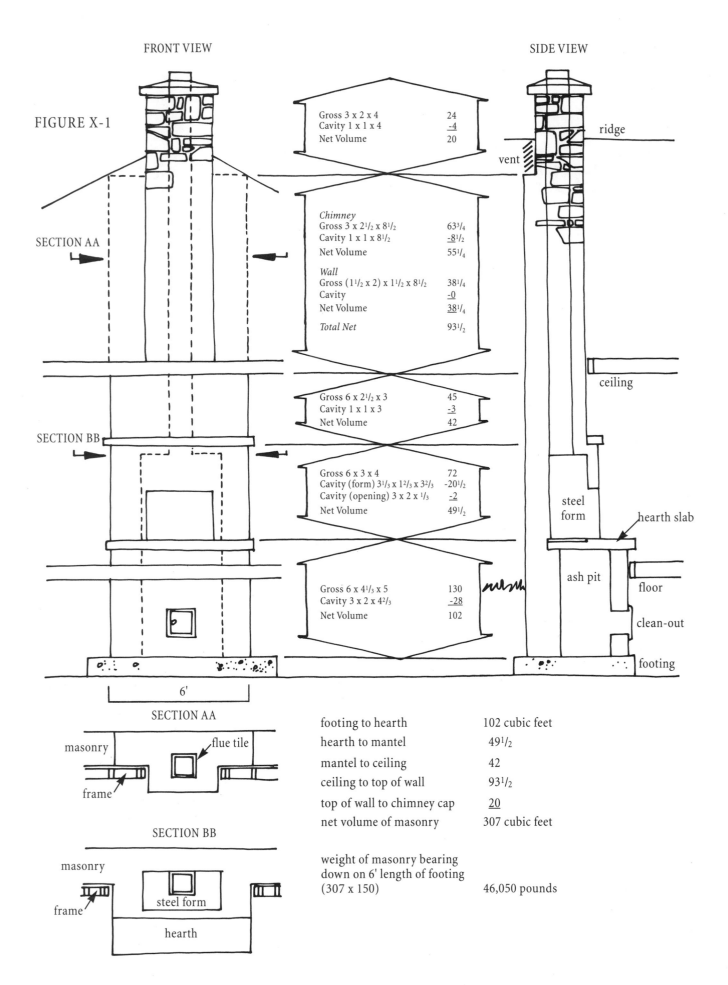

FRONT VIEW

SIDE VIEW

FIGURE X-1

SECTION AA

SECTION BB

Gross 3 x 2 x 4	24
Cavity 1 x 1 x 4	-4
Net Volume	20

Chimney

Gross 3 x 2½ x 8½	63¾
Cavity 1 x 1 x 8½	-8½
Net Volume	55¼

Wall

Gross (1½ x 2) x 1½ x 8½	38¼
Cavity	-0
Net Volume	38¼
Total Net	93½

Gross 6 x 2½ x 3	45
Cavity 1 x 1 x 3	-3
Net Volume	42

Gross 6 x 3 x 4	72
Cavity (form) 3⅓ x 1²⁄₃ x 3²⁄₃	-20½
Cavity (opening) 3 x 2 x ⅓	-2
Net Volume	49½

Gross 6 x 4⅓ x 5	130
Cavity 3 x 2 x 4²⁄₃	-28
Net Volume	102

ridge

vent

ceiling

steel
form

hearth slab

ash pit

floor

clean-out

footing

6'

SECTION AA

masonry

flue tile

frame

SECTION BB

masonry

frame

steel form

hearth

footing to hearth	102 cubic feet
hearth to mantel	49½
mantel to ceiling	42
ceiling to top of wall	93½
top of wall to chimney cap	20
net volume of masonry	307 cubic feet

weight of masonry bearing
down on 6' length of footing
(307 x 150)   46,050 pounds

for amateurs, it is only fair to warn the reader that all the assurances about the forgiving nature of stone do not apply to masonry fireplaces. Even a little mistake in a fireplace can ruin it. In the end, it is the builder's confidence in his own skills that marks the choice between steel and masonry fireplaces.

Regardless of how simple or complex the fireplace will be, the easiest way to proceed is to build in stages, one section at a time. Pour the fireplace footing with all the rest of the footings. Build the base (from footing to hearth) at the same time as the wall foundation. The fireplace itself and the lower portion of the chimney should rise at the same pace as the wall beside it. This ensures that all the masonry is properly "tied" together with overlapping stones. Even if the fireplace stands on its own, separated from the exterior wall, it is wiser for the builder to keep wall and fireplace rising at roughly the same pace. Framing, scaffolding, moving of materials, all are simplified by proceeding one stage at a time.

PLANNING

The best place to start is at the bottom, right down at the footings. Even if the fireplace is to be part of the wall, remember that there will be a great deal of extra stone involved, and the footing may have to be wider there to carry the extra weight. Begin with a rough scale drawing of the fireplace and chimney. Figure X-1 shows one example, with a large base, ash pit, raised hearth, a wide stone façade above the mantel and a chimney incorporated into an exterior wall. The object is to calculate the total weight bearing down on that 6-foot portion of footing under the fireplace.

The calculation is complicated by the fact that the masonry changes its shape several times on its way to the roof. No problem. Just calculate each section separately, and add the results together. For example, from the footing to the hearth, the overall dimensions are:

6 feet wide x 4 feet 4 inches thick x 5 feet high
= 130 cubic feet

That is the gross volume, from which we should subtract the volume of the empty ash pit. That cavity measures:

3 feet wide x 2 feet thick x 4 feet 8 inches high
= 28 cubic feet

We could also subtract the volume of the clean-out door and add the weight of the ashes, but there is really no need to be that precise. We will estimate that that section contains 102 cubic feet of masonry:

130 − 28 = 102 cubic feet net volume

Added together, the five sections shown in Figure X-1 contain a total of 307 cubic feet of masonry. That includes the foundation, the fireplace, the chimney, even the portion of the wall on either side of the chimney—everything that bears down on the 6-foot stretch of footing. At 150 pounds per cubic foot, all of that

masonry would weigh 46,050 pounds.

The footing must carry more than the masonry, however. There are the roof, the floors and the in-laws adding to the total weight. We went through all that in Chapter III, so let's skip the details here and simply say that all the extra weight amounts to 300,000 pounds for the whole house, that the footing around the perimeter is 140 feet long and that there are no central piers to help. In such a case, each linear foot along the base would have to support 2,143 pounds of in-laws and other nonmasonry extras:

$$\frac{300,000 \text{ pounds}}{140 \text{ feet}} = 2,143 \text{ pounds/linear foot}$$

and 2,143 pounds/linear foot x 6 feet = 12,858 pounds

So over that 6-foot stretch of footing, we will have 46,050 pounds of masonry and 12,858 pounds of additional weight. Add them together, and round off the sum to 60,000 pounds. That is how much will have to be supported on the fireplace footing.

The table in Chapter III indicates the bearing capacities of various soils. The total weight divided by the bearing capacity gives the area of footing required. A compact sandy subsoil, for example, has a bearing capacity of 3,000 pounds/square foot. So the hypothetical fireplace in Figure X-1 would need a footing with an area of 20 square feet:

$$\frac{60,000 \text{ pounds}}{3,000 \text{ pounds/square foot}} = \frac{20\text{-square-foot}}{\text{minimum footing area}}$$

That part of the footing is 6 feet long, thus it should be made at least 3 feet 4 inches wide. Figure X-1 shows the footing extended to a 5-foot width, a healthy margin of safety for that particular design on that particular soil.

It is impossible to generalize about how big a fireplace footing should be. It depends on the size of the house, the fireplace and the chimney. It depends on the type of soil on which the footing rests. Once you have drawn the design, however, the calculation of footing size is fairly straightforward. Find the volume, the masonry weight and the total weight, then go to the soil table to find the area of footing required.

That is the hardest part. The easy part is to pour the footing you have designed. Pour it at the same time you pour the wall footings and in just the same way.

The simplest base for a fireplace is a solid block of masonry on which the hearth, the fireplace and the chimney will rest—a wide place in the foundation, in other words. That is the most basic approach and one that the beginner can always come back to when the "optional extras" get too complicated.

There are at least two refinements that one *could* include at this stage. The first is an ash dump (shown in Figure X-1). The weight on the base is concentrated mostly at the back of the fireplace (under the chimney),

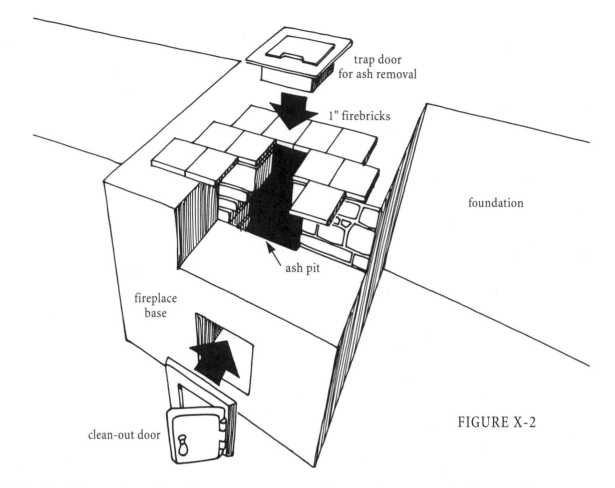

trap door
for ash removal

1" firebricks

foundation

ash pit

fireplace
base

FIGURE X-2

clean-out door

at either side of the opening and, to a lesser extent, under the hearth. The center of the base supports nothing except the grate, the logs and the firebrick floor. So little is lost if the center of the base—the core—is left hollow. A small metal trap door under the grate and a larger clean-out door beneath the floor provide a convenient way to handle ashes. Both parts are available from building-supply dealers. Mortar the clean-out door into the base. The trap door will be fitted when the firebricks are laid. The cavity itself can be any convenient size or shape, so long as it does not undermine the essential solid masonry under the back and sides of the fireplace.

Another optional refinement is a duct to bring air into the combustion chamber from outside the house. Most fireplaces use warm inside air to supply the fire. As the warm air goes up the chimney, cold air is drawn into the house to replace it. The icy drafts continue even after the fire dies down. The air duct allows cooler outside air to feed the blaze, while the warm air stays in the house. Installation is simple enough if you think of it *before* the exterior wall is built. Leave a hole through the wall at a point somewhere below the fireplace. (Methods of building holes in the wall are discussed in Chapter III. Clay drainage tiles or a section of wide metal pipe—laid right into the wall like a long, skinny stone—would leave an adequate air passage.) Mortar a screened vent into

the outside opening. The duct goes through the fireplace base and emerges in the front, central portion of the fire area. This opening in the hearth has to be fitted with another metal door or grate, which will be added when the firebricks are laid. Some prefab fireplace units include an exterior vent and a hearth vent for this purpose.

THE HEARTH

The simplest hearth is made by covering a solid base with a layer of flat stone slabs. The hearth should extend out 18 inches from where the fireplace opening will be and should reach a minimum of 8 inches beyond each side of the opening. The floor of the fire area itself should be covered with a layer of 1-inch firebrick (unprotected stone might crack in the heat). The firebrick floor should be set in a bed of fire clay, or refractory cement, sold especially for this purpose. Alternatively, the mason can use a rich mortar (1 part cement to 2 parts sand) of Portland cement. Lime mortars should not be used, and the Portland mortar should be used only where it will not be exposed directly to the fire.

Where the base is not solid but has been left hollow to form an ash dump, it will be necessary to cap the top of the hole before laying the hearth. Over a small cavity, it may be enough to taper in the last few courses of stone

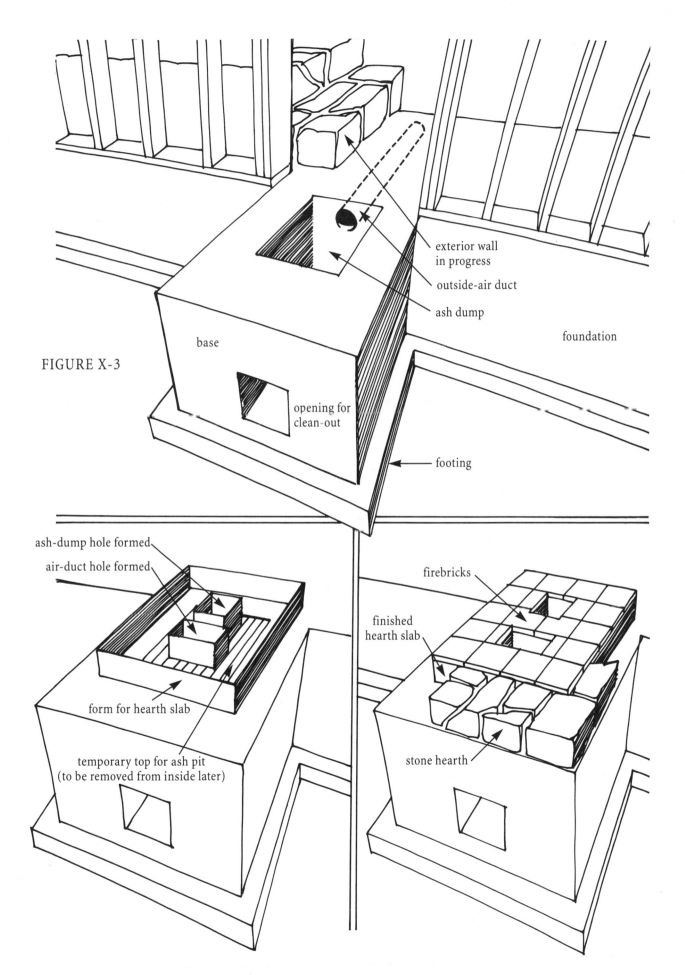

FIGURE X-3

exterior wall
in progress

outside-air duct

ash dump

foundation

base

opening for
clean-out

footing

ash-dump hole formed

air-duct hole formed

firebricks

finished
hearth slab

form for hearth slab

temporary top for ash pit
(to be removed from inside later)

stone hearth

Fireplaces & Chimneys

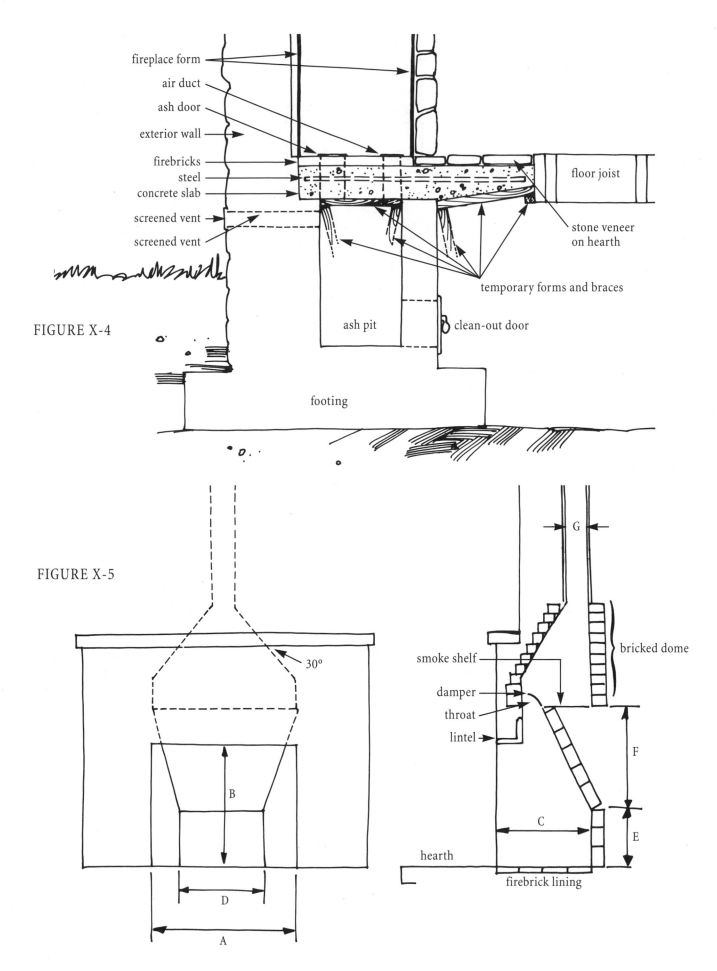

fireplace form

air duct

ash door

exterior wall

firebricks

steel

concrete slab

screened vent

screened vent

floor joist

stone veneer
on hearth

temporary forms and braces

FIGURE X-4

ash pit

clean-out door

footing

FIGURE X-5

G

30°

bricked dome

smoke shelf

damper

throat

lintel

B

C

F

E

hearth

D

firebrick lining

A

until the hole at the top is the same size as the prefab trap door (as shown in the cutaway section of Figure X-2). Fit the firebricks around the rim of the hole, and insert the trap door.

Larger cavities will need a more solid top. The usual method is to cap the base with a concrete slab. The top of the hole is filled with boards braced from underneath. Then a form is built for the slab, and smaller forms are set inside the larger one to leave holes for the trap door and the air duct. Steel rods and mesh can be worked into the concrete to reinforce it. When the concrete has set, the boards that closed the top of the hole are removed by reaching up through the clean-out door. The hardest part is getting the boards and braces out through the ash pit afterward. The alternative is to fill up the cavity with sand, then shovel it out later. Top the slab with firebricks inside and stone on the hearth. And plan the forming of the slab with the thickness of the hearth stones in mind in order to finish the two surfaces at the same height.

The Cadillac of hearth slabs is the cantilevered model shown in Figure X-4. The procedure is similar to that shown in X-3, except that the cantilevered hearth means that you can get away with building a much narrower base. Forms and braces get a little trickier, and the steel reinforcing is a must.

The novice mason has a wide range of choices. You can support the hearth on a solid base of stone, cheap and easy cement blocks or a sophisticated base of concrete, steel and ductwork. The time, budget and skill of the builder determine the method. And regardless of how you arrived at the hearth, at this point, you still have a choice between a masonry fireplace and the factory-built steel form. Let's look at the easy way first.

THE PREFAB FIREPLACE

There are a number of different models on the market, and you should follow the manufacturer's instructions for its specific unit. Most, however, are installed something like this:

1. Set the fireplace form on the hearth. Position it exactly where you want it, making sure that the floor of the combustion area is fully firebricked and that you leave at least 18 inches of hearth in front of the fireplace opening.

2. Add the ducts that will lead from the heat exchanger to the room. There are usually four of these—two to bring in cold air from near the floor and two hot-air vents near the top of the unit. The hot-air vents can be directed from the face or the sides of the fireplace or into an adjacent room. Although it is possible to build smoothly parged ducts right into the stonework, you may find it easier to form the ducts from sheet metal (galvanized flashing metal works well and is readily available). Keep the inside dimensions of the duct the same as the hole where it joins the fireplace form. End the duct just where you want it to emerge from the masonry.

3. Some units have fans to push air through the heat exchanger more quickly. If the fan is to be hidden inside the duct, now is the time to get the wiring in place.

4. Put a ½-inch blanket of fireproof insulation around the outside of the form where the steel would come in contact with the masonry. The purpose is to leave room for the steel to expand without cracking the masonry.

5. Now start laying stone around the form. The jambs (either side of the opening) carry the weight, so make them fairly broad—no less than half the width of the opening itself. Thus, if your fireplace is to have a 36-inch opening, there should be 18 inches of stone on either side. At the front of the form, around the opening, you will have to use slimmer (almost veneer) stones. Don't make the masonry thinner than 4 inches, though.

6. When you reach a duct, just build right around it. Bridge across the top of the ducts with larger stones, and mortar in the vent at the end of the duct where it emerges from the face of the stonework. These vents are often supplied with the form.

7. Most manufacturers recommend a steel lintel across the top of the fireplace opening. A well-made arch would do just as well. A good arch on a steel lintel would be even better.

8. Another steel angle may be needed at the top of some units where the chimney starts. Add the steel according to the instructions for your particular model.

Width of opening	Height of opening	Depth to back	Width of back	Height of vertical back wall	Height of sloping back wall	Inside diameter of flue
A	B	C	D	E	F	G
24	24	16	14	14	18	10
30	28	16	16	14	22	10
36	30	18	22	14	24	12
42	30	18	28	14	24	12
48	32	20	32	14	26	15

Measurements are in inches

FIGURE X-6

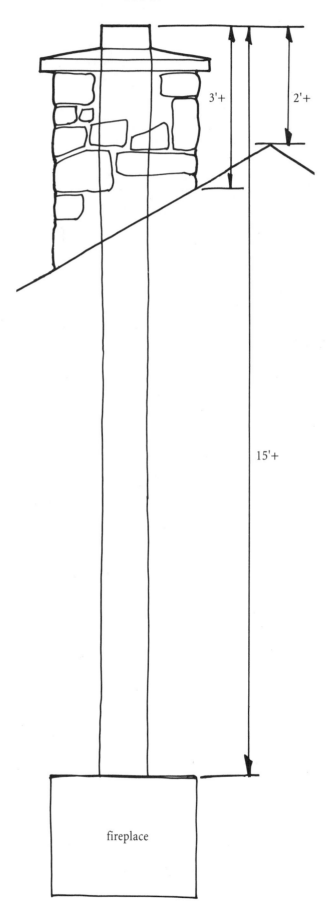

3'+

2'+

15'+

fireplace

That's it. The mantel shelf, alcoves and other extras are strictly matters of taste. With the forms, a fireplace is simply a stone face with preset openings. Everything else but the chimney is an optional extra.

Although the installation procedures are fairly standard, the product itself does vary from manufacturer to manufacturer. Shop around for the right design as well as the right price. Some models offer ribbing or extra reinforcement on the back panel of the firebox, where warpage from heat can be a problem. Another design has a masonry coating over the smoke shelf to keep it from rusting prematurely. Some models are made with heavier-gauge steel than are others (although any steel plate will warp if it gets hot enough).

The traditional, made-from-scratch masonry fireplace goes up in more or less the same order as the prefab job. The major difference is that the builder forms the innards himself—from brick. And, no, that is not really trifling with the integrity of an all-stone building. In the first place, intense heat will crack and destroy most stones. Secondly, the inner proportions and angles are much too exacting for the rough-and-ready approach of fieldstone.

The proper proportions for the those innards are a matter of some dispute. Every craftsman has his own approach. Even the codes and "official" tables disagree. The table on page 109 shows some sample dimensions, amalgamated from several published sources. Figure X-5 illustrates the parts of the fireplace to which the measurements apply.

Regardless of whose proportions you choose to follow, there are a few general rules that seem to be widely accepted:

1. The vertical distance from the lintel to the throat should be no less than 8 inches.

2. The area of the throat should be no less than the cross-sectional area of the flue.

3. The smoke shelf should be at least 10 inches deep.

4. Both the smoke shelf and the throat should be as wide as the fireplace opening.

Almost 200 years ago, Count Rumford recognized that the heating efficiency of a masonry fireplace depended primarily on the radiant heat of the fire—direct radiance plus the heat reflected from the back of the fireplace into the room. Rumford designed a fireplace with a very shallow firebox, a tall opening and sharply slanted sides to reflect more heat into the room. He narrowed the throat to 4 inches to maintain the draft required to keep smoke from wafting out of the shallow firebox.

As the fireplace gave way to stoves, furnaces and then electric heat, modern designers ignored the question of heat efficiency and began building the squat, deep-backed fireplace that is most common in houses today. The modern fireplace is less likely to smoke in a tightly sealed house and much less likely to provide any useful

Setting the first tile in the chimney straight, plumb and square is the best way to begin (LEFT). *An air space* (RIGHT) *should be left between the tile and the surrounding masonry.*

heat, when compared to the Rumford design.

The Rumford fireplace is coming back into vogue among those who want a fireplace for warmth as well as looks. Its critical features are:

1. The opening is as high as it is wide.

2. The depth of the firebox is $\frac{1}{3}$ the opening width.

3. The back wall is only as wide as the firebox is deep.

4. The throat is as wide as the opening but only 4 inches deep.

Just for the sake of comparison, a Rumford fireplace that is 36 inches wide would be 36 inches high and 12 inches deep, with the back wall (the vertical part) 12 inches by 12 inches. Contrast that with the conventional 36-inch fireplace in the table on page 109.

Choose the dimensions and proportions that suit you best, but do make sure that the fireplace has a smoke dome, a smoke shelf and a damper. Follow the general rules cited above, and check your local building code. Some codes will not even allow the Rumford fireplace, despite its recognized efficiency. And that says more about building codes than it does about fireplaces.

Make several scale drawings of the fireplace plan. You will need the drawings to plot the various angles correctly and to calculate the number of bricks to order. The guts of the fireplace will be built in two distinct stages: the fire chamber (from the hearth to the throat) and the smoke chamber (from the throat to the chimney). Each stage is built from the inside out. In other words, the inner lining is erected first and the stone shell added afterward.

The process begins just where we started with the steel-form fireplace—with the base and hearth completed and the fire-chamber floor covered with a 1-inch layer of firebricks. The ash dump and outside-air duct (if included) will already be in place.

The first step is to build the actual fire chamber from 2-inch firebrick. The side walls slant in toward the back, so the back wall will be narrower than the front opening. Mark the position of the back wall and the sides on the firebrick floor. Setting the 2-inch bricks on edge, assemble the first course dry (without mortar). Because the side walls meet the back at an angle, the ends of the side-wall bricks will have to be beveled to make a snug joint. Mark the cut on the brick, and use a masonry blade in the power saw to trim it off.

Now set the first course in a bed of refractory cement. Joints should be thin, $\frac{1}{4}$ inch or less, and should be given a smooth, flush pointing. The three walls rise vertically for several courses until you reach the point where the

A clean-out door at the bottom of the chimney makes ash removal easy. The door is mortared in as part of the wall.

which forms the fourth wall of the upper part of the fire chamber, the inside surface should be smoothly parged.

With the whole structure complete to the throat, mortar in the damper unit (which most masons will buy prebuilt), and smooth out the smoke shelf behind it. Now, with ordinary bricks and Portland mortar, build the smoke dome. The back wall starts at the back of the smoke shelf and rises vertically. The side walls rise vertically for several courses until they are clear of the damper. Then the front and side walls slope inward to meet the flue. This slope should be no more than 30 degrees from the vertical and can be formed by offsetting each course of brick an inch or less toward the center, like an inverted staircase. A wall that leans at an angle like that sounds rickety, but as long as the corner bricks overlap and as long as you avoid continuous vertical joints, the pyramid will not collapse.

The inside surface of the smoke dome should be parged. Do this with each course, or reach in through the hole at the top when the dome is complete. Either way, the construction and parging of the dome can be a messy business. Cover the damper and the smoke shelf with a feed sack or something to catch the falling mortar.

The hole at the top of the smoke dome should coincide exactly with the inside dimensions of the flue liner. The last course of brick forms a ledge to support the liner, but it should not extend beyond the rim of the liner into the flue space.

Now encase the dome with stone, add a mantel to complete the face, and the fireplace is finished. The last stage—the chimney—is the same whether the fireplace is formed with factory steel or hand-fitted brick.

The chimney, like the fireplace, is built from the inside out. You start with the lining, then add the shell. For both permanence and performance, the chimney should be lined with specially fired clay flue tiles. These are sold by most building-supply dealers and come in a variety of sizes and shapes. It is most important to choose a tile with a cross-sectional area matched to the size of the stove or fireplace it will be serving. If you are buying a prefab fireplace form or a woodstove, the dealer should be able to tell you exactly what size flue it requires. For masonry fireplaces, refer to the table on page 109 for sample dimensions. The flue dimensions in the table are for round tiles. If you are buying square or rectangular tiles, just remember that they are slightly less efficient than the round ones (the smoke doesn't use the corners) and the flue areas do not correspond exactly. For example, the 36-by-30-inch fireplace takes a 12-inch round tile (with an area of 114 square inches), but the same fireplace would need a 12-by-12-inch square tile (144 square inches). The square tiles seem to be more popular with dealers, perhaps because they are easier to stack and handle. The standard tile is 2 feet long.

Plan the chimney carefully to avoid later problems

back wall starts to slope forward, toward the fireplace opening. Keep the angle of the slope uniform by laying the back-wall bricks against a wooden template or guide (simply a scrap of plywood cut to match the angles of the floor, the vertical back and the sloping back).

When the back wall starts its slope, the abutting side bricks will have to be cut on a double bevel. Some masons recommend an adjustable square to mark the bevels. Others stack up the side walls dry and mark the intersecting angle of the back wall with a board and chalk. Regardless of how the cuts are marked, this is where the masonry blade comes into its own. The cuts are finicky enough without hacking around with hammer and chisel, trying to cut a double bevel.

The three-walled structure ends at the throat. Before you go any further with the innards, start at the hearth again and encase the firebrick structure with stone. The stone shell may be much larger than the firebrick chamber, extending from the outside of the wall to the finished face of the fireplace. Fill any spaces between the stone face and the firebrick with mortared rubble. Set in the steel lintel at the top of the fireplace opening, and build up the face of the fireplace above it. Behind this face,

FIGURE X-7

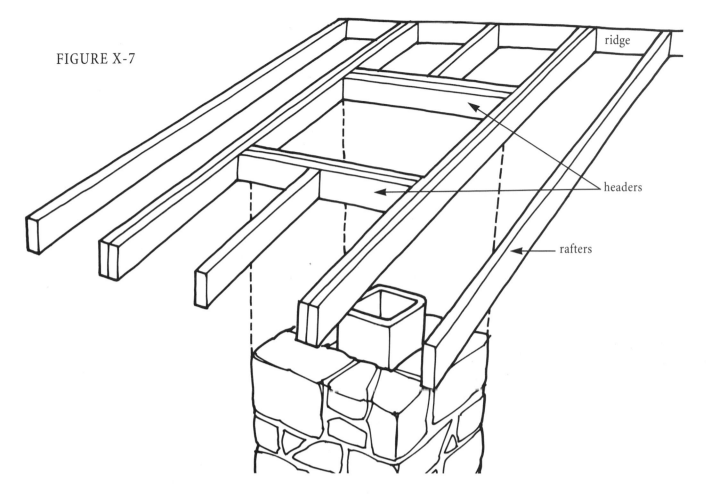

ridge

headers

rafters

with smoke. The ideal plan is to place the chimney so that it emerges from the roof at the ridge. Any breeze is deflected upward there and tends to pull the smoke out of the hole rather than stuffing it back in. If you have to miss the ridge, the top of the chimney should still be at least 2 feet higher than the ridge or 2 feet higher than anything else within 10 feet of the chimney. In either case, the top of the flue must be at least 3 feet higher than the nearest roof surface (Figure X-6). Finally, the distance from the fireplace opening to the top of the flue should be at least 15 feet if the fireplace is to draw properly. The taller the chimney, the better the draft.

The fireplace, remember, has been completed to the top of the smoke chamber. If you have used a steel form, that is the hole in the top. If the steel form is accompanied by instructions that call for additional steel or masonry supports for the chimney, now is the time to install them.

Lay a bed of Portland mortar around the edge of the hole, and set the first tile firmly in the mortar. It may take some tapping and shimming, but every effort should be made to seat the tile squarely over the hole and to ensure that it is perfectly plumb. Now, reaching in from the top, smooth any mortar that might have been squeezed from the joint. There should be no projections on which soot and creosote could collect.

With the tile in place, the stone shell of the chimney is built around it. Not solidly *against* it, though. Right at the joint, it helps to set a few rocks against the tile just to hold it in place. But subsequent courses, above the joint, should leave air pockets between the stone and the tile. Some masons wrap the tile with a thin batt of insulation, just as you did the fireplace form. I find, however, that the rough back sides of the fieldstone never fit solidly against the smoother tiles. As long as I'm not too sloppy with the mortar, the necessary gaps between stone and tile occur quite naturally. The purpose of the air space is to insulate the flue and allow for heat expansion. It is supposed to heat up faster and draw more easily that way.

There should be a minimum of 4 inches of solid masonry around all sides of the tile; so a single 8-by-12-inch flue would result in a chimney measuring 16 inches by 20 inches by the time you got it covered with stone. And that is an absolute minimum. With a tall chimney or rough stones, you will want to build it considerably wider. If the chimney contains more than one flue (every burning unit should have its own flue), keep them separated with at least 3 inches of masonry between them.

Lay up the stonework right to the top of each tile. Then put a bead of mortar around the tile rim, and set the next tile on it. Be sure it lines up squarely with the

FIGURE X-8

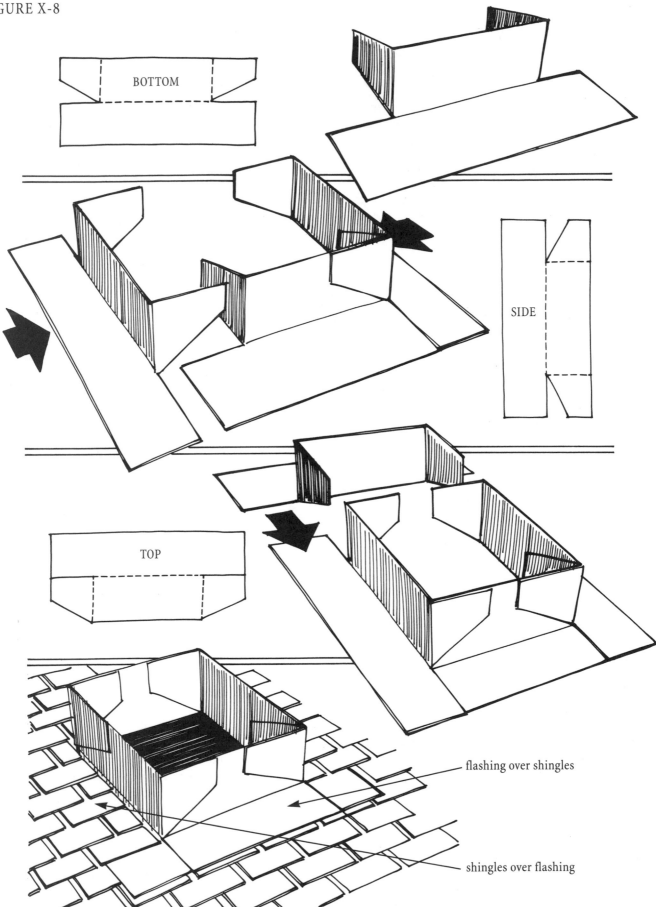

BOTTOM

SIDE

TOP

flashing over shingles

shingles over flashing

FIGURE X-9

lower tile, and use a level to check the vertical alignment. As the chimney rises higher, a plumb bob and string will give you a more accurate vertical check. Again, reach in from the top, and smooth out any excess mortar. Place just enough stone and mortar around the outside to keep the tile from being knocked out of place. Bring the stone shell up to the top, and add another tile.

Setting the tiles inevitably results in a shower of mortar down the flue. Some masons recommend a burlap bag partially filled with sand, sawdust or straw. Tie a rope on the bag, and stuff it into the first tile. When a higher tile is added and solidly blocked into place, the bag is drawn up past the joint and brings all the wasted mortar with it. Nice theory. I still end up trying to clean out the garbage from the bottom. Just in case the bag trick doesn't work for you either, leave some plastic sheeting or loose bags on the smoke shelf so that the falling mortar will at least not stick to the shelf when it falls. These bags, or whatever, will have to be removed through the damper when the job is finished.

Cleaning off a smoke shelf by reaching up through the damper is the world's second nastiest job. Even if you can keep the mortar off it, the smoke shelf will eventually collect soot, birds and other debris. Sooner or later, it will have to be cleaned. Our first fireplace had to be cleaned through the damper. It is possible—but not without a skinned elbow, a faceful of soot and a new vocabulary for the children. The second chimney included a "clean-out," a hole through the outside wall, just below the bottom tile. It includes a cast-iron door, just like the clean-out door for an ash pit.

The trickiest part of building a chimney is to get it safely through the roof. It takes some planning to keep the heat in the chimney and the rain on the roof. Heat protection is obtained by leaving a 2-inch gap between the chimney and any adjacent framing—in this case, the rafters. Any rafters that would pass through the chimney space have to be interrupted and braced to the full rafters on either side with "headers" (Figure X-7). The simplest way to proceed is to frame and sheathe the roof first, leaving a hole where the chimney is to pass through. Then build the chimney up through the hole. A plumb bob dropped from the corners of the roof hole helps to establish the limits of the chimney and keeps it rising vertically. When the masonry reaches the rafters, you can use a spacer to keep the stone 2 inches away from the wood.

That 2-inch safety gap leads, in turn, to the water problem: how to keep it from taking the shortcut through the gap and down the front of your fireplace. The answer is to close the gap with metal flashing. Building-supply stores sell rolls of flashing material in aluminum or galvanized metal (sometimes copper in the high-rent district). The flashing can be cut with common tin snips and bent by clamping the metal

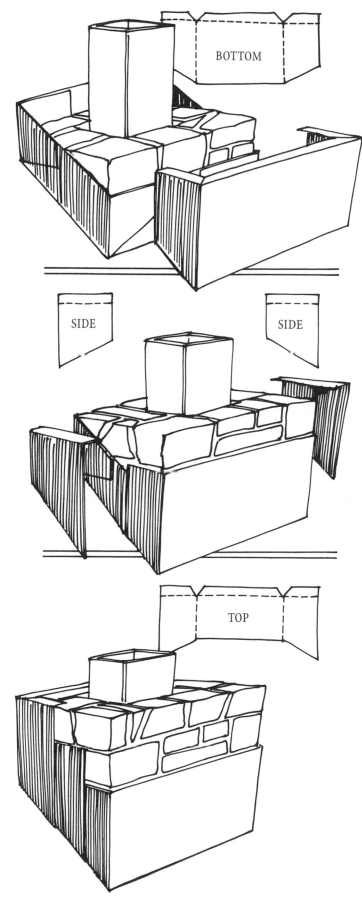

Height, distance from the ridge, prevailing wind, even the surrounding trees affect the draft from a chimney flue.

between two straight boards and using a third board or a wooden mallet to crease the metal. Figure X-8 shows the four pieces needed to form the base flashing for a square chimney in the middle of a roof. The angle of the cutouts depends on the pitch of the roof. You will have to custom-fit the flashing to your own roof slope. Figure X-8 merely illustrates the process. The base flashing is most easily installed at the time the shingles are applied. As you can see, the flashing is included in the pattern of overlapping, just as if it were part of the shingles. The base flashing is cut to fit the chimney, not the hole in the roof (which, of course, is 2 inches larger than the chimney). The flashing is fastened down with roofing nails, and the overlapping portions are stuck together with roofing cement. Clamps may be needed to keep the tabs in place while the roofing cement hardens.

Now build the rest of the chimney up through the hole, setting the masonry snugly against the flashing and 2 inches away from the wood. As the masonry emerges from the hole, you should add counter-flashing at each course. The counter-flashing is buried in the mortar joints, then comes down over the side of the masonry to overlap the base flashing (Figure X-9).

If you are ever tempted to cheat and use bricks or blocks instead of stones, this is the place to do it. Straight, regular courses will take most of the frustration out of fitting the counter-flashing.

Cut the bottom piece of counter-flashing to fit the first course of masonry that rises above the base flashing. Be sure to leave a couple of extra inches at the top to bend over into the mortar joint. Stick the tabs to the base flashing with roofing cement. Now lay another course of stones on the chimney. The first set of side pieces goes from the top of this course to the roof. Again, the tab is stuck to the base flashing with roofing

cement. Another course of stone follows, then another set of side pieces, and so on, until you reach the back corner of the chimney. The top piece of counter-flashing goes on last, with its ends bent around to look like two more side pieces.

The metal can be awkward and floppy, and the overlaps don't always stick together neatly. Roofing cement hardens slowly, so go ahead and complete the flashing, adding at least one more course of stone above the last section of counter-flashing. *Then* you can go back and restick all the floppy bits that didn't stay in place with the cement. It may even help to put a board on each side of the chimney and clamp the side pieces in place until the cement hardens. Alternatively, use pop rivets or solder to join the pieces.

Once you are safely through the roof, the hardest part is getting the stones up to the mason. Simply continue with tiles and stone until the top of the last tile is at least 2 feet higher than the ridge. The draft is improved if you leave 6 inches of bare tile above the last course of stones.

Save the best uniformly flat slabs for the final course. These are set to project an inch or so beyond the face of the masonry below, then the top is carefully troweled smooth and sloped from the tile to the edge. The purpose is to form a cap that will shed rain rather than allow it to run down the sides of the chimney. If acrophobia is affecting your trowel hand, you can always buy or make a precast concrete cap, with a hole in the center to fit over the flue tile.

Clean up the last of any mess that might have fallen down the chimney, and leave it to cure for at least a month before lighting any fires. A real Scots mason (or any other Scot with a glass in his hand) would now wish you well with a favorite toast: "Lang mae yer lum reek!" or long may your chimney smoke.

*Masonry styles can be adapted to most purposes, even
when the purpose is just the whimsical joy of building.*

THE STONEBUILDER'S PRIMER

XI Variations

We shape our buildings;

thereafter they shape us.

— *Winston Churchill*

OUR OWN APPROACH to building in stone—a traditional face with a formed back and air space—is the product of particular circumstances. It suits the type of stone available and does not exceed our limited skills. Other builders in other circumstances might well find other techniques more suitable.

For reasons of ease and economy, we still prefer the method we first used for the house. Since that time, however, we have dabbled with some alternatives that have advantages of their own.

TRADITIONAL

A solid wall of stone with two finished faces seems to be an extravagant use of time and material when you realize that the inner face will have to be covered with insulation anyway. For outbuildings, however, where insulation is unnecessary, the two-faced wall is an economical alternative. You don't have to buy lumber until you get to the roof. This is a particularly attractive approach on bedrock, where the usual footings and foundations are unnecessary. Here, a small stone building can go up almost as quickly and cheaply as a wooden one.

The woodshed wall was built this way. Insulation was unnecessary, bedrock was at the bottom of a shallow trench, and a packed earth floor was all that was required inside. We cleaned out the trench and filled it with concrete; it could have been stone, but concrete was faster. Starting at ground level on the concrete base, the wall (24 feet by 5 feet by 16 inches) was finished in five working days. Two guide strings were used, one for each face of the wall. And because the wall was somewhat thinner than the traditional solid wall, some care had to be taken to fit each face stone so that it did not interfere with the back end of the stone on the opposite face. Even so, it went up almost as quickly as other walls built against a spacer/form. Our only regret was the rapid depletion of the carefully hoarded pile of good face stones. We had a large and solid woodshed for the cost of the lumber to roof it, but the next spring found us back in the rock pile scrounging for more good face stones.

Apart from the double string and faces, the traditional wall goes up in exactly the same way as described in Chapter VII. Fitting, mortar, bridging joints, bonding units, pointing—the traditional wall follows the same procedures.

Someone tried to improve the looks of this old solid stone building by adding a modern veneer.

VENEER

When we began the log house, we thought we could save time by starting with the usual concrete-block foundation. It could easily be covered later with a stone veneer. That was the theory. And as usual, practice shot a few holes in the theory.

Gathering stones for a veneer is more time-consuming than finding stone for a solid wall. Granted, veneer requires less stone than a solid wall does, but shaping and fitting are so much more important in veneer construction that the search for the right piece takes longer. In a solid wall, the stones are normally laid flat. Odd protrusions and irregular shapes can be hidden in the middle of the wall or left to protrude from the face. Veneer requires that the stone have a flat back side (to fit snugly against the existing wall) and a flat face (too much protrusion would overbalance a stone that is set on edge) and still be square enough around the edges to form the tight joints that are essential when the wall is as thin as 3 to 4 inches. Unless you have access to some exceptionally good stones, a long search and considerable cutting are involved in fieldstone veneers.

Only after we had built a few solid walls of stone did we realize that we could have laid up a solid stone foundation with less time and effort than the veneer demanded. Even worse is the realization that the veneer still looks like veneer—in marked contrast to the real stone walls beside it. If you are still interested, the procedure goes something like this:

The backup wall (the real wall behind the veneer) must first be fitted with ties. These are corrugated metal straps that literally tie the veneer to the backup wall. If the backup wall is wooden frame, simply nail the ties to the studs. If the backup wall is block or brick, the ties should be built right into the mortar joints, with one end left sticking out. In either case, space the ties about 16 inches apart vertically (that's every other course with the standard 8-inch block) and about 30 inches horizontally.

With the backup wall liberally studded with these metal tassels, start the veneer from the footings or from the top of the foundation if a ledge has been provided there. Use a good masonry cement, and apply the mortar to the block wall behind the veneer as well as to the edges of adjacent veneer stones. When you reach a tie, bend it to fit the nearest joint and bury it in the mortar.

When applying veneer to a wood-frame wall, remember that masonry and wood are best kept apart. Leave an air space between the veneer and the wall, or use an impermeable barrier between them.

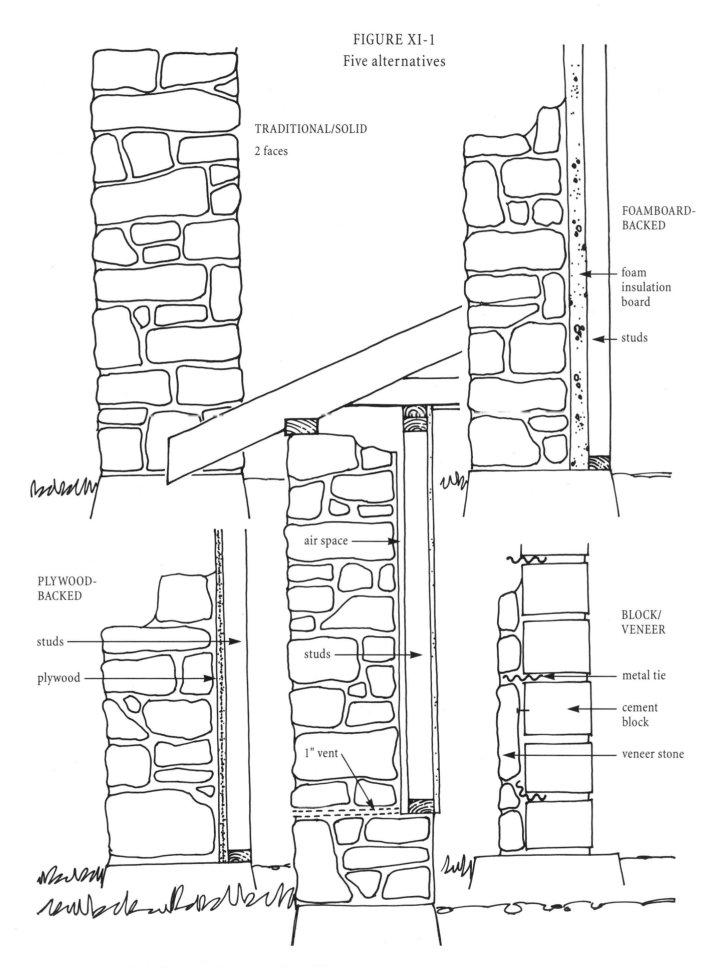

FIGURE XI-1
Five alternatives

TRADITIONAL/SOLID
2 faces

FOAMBOARD-
BACKED

foam
insulation
board

studs

PLYWOOD-
BACKED

studs

plywood

air space

studs

1" vent

BLOCK/
VENEER

metal tie

cement
block

veneer stone

Remember, too, that a wood-frame wall is always subject to some degree of flexing. Temperature changes, winds and even movement on the floors will flex a wooden wall. When the wall is tied to a more rigid stone veneer, there are bound to be disputes and perhaps even violence. Like any mixed marriage, it can work if carefully built, but on the face of it, stone against block would seem to be a more reliable match for the beginner.

Setting all those stones on edge is a balancing act. The higher and thinner the wall, the less reliable it is. The standards issued by the National Research Council insist that a masonry veneer 3 inches thick should go no higher than 9 feet at the eaves (measured from the base, not from ground level). A thicker veneer is allowed to rise higher, but these official limits are based on standard masonry units (that is, bricks and blocks). If the field-stone you are using is somewhat more wobbly on its edge than a brick would be, make the veneer correspondingly thicker and lower than the limits set by your building code.

ALTERNATIVES TO THE AIR SPACE

When we pull out the spacer/form at the back of a freshly laid course of stone, it leaves a narrow air space behind the wall. The idea is to prevent the insulation and the studs of the inner wall from touching the masonry, which takes dampness from the air like a sponge.

Air is not the only answer to the moisture problem, though. Waterproof barriers, such as rigid foam panels, can work. And some builders have even ignored the moisture altogether, albeit with mixed success.

Doug, a fellow amateur mason, built his inner walls first, then sheathed them with plywood and moved into the house. Now he's building a granite wall that is mortared solidly against the plywood—no air space at all. He adds the granite in dribs and drabs, and the plywood has allowed them to live comfortably behind the half-stoned walls for eight years. Our approach, on the other hand, left the space unroofed and uninhabitable until the stonework was complete.

The moisture, however, is beginning to exact its toll. Doug now finds that the plywood backing is starting to rot behind the stones. The effect on the insulation and framing remains to be seen.

We're trying another variation on this approach with the smokehouse. The inner frame was clad with ¼-inch untreated chipboard. This material is not at all water-resistant. It disintegrates in the dew. Still, we wanted to operate the smokehouse for a couple of seasons with cheap temporary walls—just to get the kinks out of the essential pipes and vents. When it was all functioning properly, the walls were committed to stone. We covered the chipboard on the outside with waterproof tar paper ("15-pound building paper," if you are asking at the supply yard). This provides the only barrier between masonry and untreated wood. Under normal circumstances, I wouldn't expect the studs and chipboard to last very long.

A cardinal rule for insulating any heated space is to put the vapor barrier on the *warm* side of the wall. Warm, moist air is stopped at the vapor barrier, and the moisture remains a gas. If that same air is allowed to pass through the insulation and reach the colder outside wall before being stopped, the moisture will condense on the colder surface and soak the insulation, the studs and everything else inside the wall. Putting the tar paper on the outside of the smokehouse and leaving no other vapor barrier inside is a violation of the usual order of things. In theory, condensation will occur between the tar paper and the chipboard, rotting the chipboard and eventually the studs. In practice, we aren't that worried, since the space is heated for only a few days a year. The rest of the time, it is an unheated storage shed, and the inside air is as cold as the stones (ergo, no condensation). If the experiment fails, we can always tear out the rotten chipboard walls from the inside and make do with a solid stone smokehouse. That, however, is the kind of remedy that would not be practical in a house. Such experiments should be restricted to the less important outbuildings without full insulation and *inside* vapor barriers.

One final variation that may prove better suited to housing is the use of rigid foam panels. These are simply glued to the outside of the studs. The foam serves as both insulation and vapor barrier. It eliminates the need for the spacer/form at the back of the masonry, since the stones can be laid right against the foamboard. Because the foam is impervious to water, no air space is needed. Because the foam is insulating, its inner surface will remain almost as warm as the room air and condensation should not form.

We considered using foam when the house was built but finally discarded the idea because of the cost and the safety problem. The white foam panels most commonly available at that time give off a toxic gas when exposed to high temperatures. We used them under the stone floors, but where fires could occur—in the walls, for example—white foam was too risky. Now foam panels are available that are approved for use in regular construction, provided they are covered with a fire-resistant material (such as Gyproc).

Using the foam panels is easy. Just glue them to the outside of the studs, making sure that the panel edges abut on a stud and not between the studs. For safety's sake, a fire-retardant material could be used between the studs and the foam. Caulk the joints between panels, and start laying stone against them. Go gently, though—foam panels can crumble and break if handled roughly.

Rigid foam may be easy to use but remains a rela-

When the weight is carried on the stone, the frame can be built in any fashion. This wall was framed with shelves, with foam insulation added on the outside, then the stone.

tively expensive form of insulation. For example, 5½ inches of fiberglass is rated R20 and sells for 34 cents per square foot. Four inches of rigid foam adds up to R20, but costs rise to more than $2 per square foot for the same R value.

Just as an experiment—an expensive experiment—one wall of the workshop was built with foam panels rather than with the spacer forms. That same wall also illustrates one last advantage of building with stone.

FRAMING VARIATIONS

When stone walls hold up the floor and the roof, the inner frame has no function but to house the insulation and wiring and to support the plaster. Standard 2-by-4 or 2-by-6 framing may be useful for housing the desired

thickness of insulation but is much more than is really needed to fulfill its minor structural role. The imaginative stonebuilder is free to do just about anything with the framing that suits his fancy.

The foam-insulated wall in the workshop, for example. Since foam was used on the outside, the space between the studs wasn't required for holding the insulation. In fact, the framing wasn't needed for holding anything except the shape of the wall and for something to protect the foam. So in place of studs, we used framing members of rough-sawn 1-by-8 lumber and ran them horizontally instead of vertically. It supported and protected the foam, formed the back of the stonework and left a handy set of built-in shelves for the inner wall.

With the weight supported on the stone, the builder can choose to frame with 2-by-2s, plank walls or the backs of kitchen cupboards. The strength of the stone will compensate for any heresy the amateur commits in the framing. As long as the frame is plumb, the stone will rise vertically beside it. Then gravity will hold the stones in place, and the stone will hold everything else.

*The essence of being an amateur is to do a thing for the joy
of it and to enjoy the thing you have done.*

XII Epilogue

Gather moss.

—Charles Long

LIKE EVERYTHING ELSE, this book must have an end. The final photographs were taken one scorching summer day when the publisher called "time," and Liz and I downed tools to celebrate the end of the book with a dip in Hazel's pool. My skin was sizzled and muscles ached from the race to finish the niche and some other odds and ends before the photographer wrapped it up. It took a while, then, before the pool and I reached an equilibrium temperature and I surfaced for an ale to cool off the insides too. Hazel and husband Bud were curious. "So your house is finally finished?" Hazel and Bud aren't stonebuilders. The question took me by surprise.

"No, of course not. The book's finished, not the house."

"When will the house be finished?"

"Uh . . . never . . . I hope."

Then, realizing that answer must sound absurd to people who think of stones as merely heavy things that have to be hauled away or whipper-snipped around, I slipped underwater again and tried to compose a more sensible reply to a perfectly normal question. When will the house be done? And why hadn't the question occurred to me before? Actually, part of the place is finished. Not the woodwork, and the cupboards aren't

up, but those are the final trimmings. The important part of the main house—the stonework—is done. We've been living in it for several years. The woodshed is done. The workshop is nearly finished. But all the stonework isn't finished, and with any luck, it never will be. When we get to the top of the workshop chimney, there's the veranda to start, a greenhouse, garage, garden walls . . . the list of projects will keep expanding. I've promised Liz she can have the mortar mixer bronzed someday, but secretly, I know I'll keep it going for a long, long time to come.

Stonebuilding does that to people. Dan Maruska, who took most of the photographs, never asked when the house would be done. The question probably never occurred to him either. He soon left the camera swinging in the apple tree and got himself elbow-deep in mortar and rocks. Like watching a jigsaw puzzle being done, it's hard to stand by for long without trying just one piece . . . and then another. The satisfaction is in the doing, not in seeing it done. At times, it comes close to therapy. Maybe it was all those years of working in offices, where the closest one comes to physical satisfaction at work is an empty "in" tray at the end of the day. To spend a day in the sun, with something real to show

125

Like seeing a jigsaw puzzle half done, it's hard to watch for long without trying just one piece—and then another.

for the effort, something that can be touched and seen, something that serves both function and beauty, something that will not change in a turbulent world, all that makes the builder glow with the joy of creation.

Moreover, it is a pleasure that even a complete novice can quickly find. The beauty, you see, is mostly in the stone. The mason merely composes it, assembling the pieces to suit his purpose. Professional skills may be necessary to build great works of beauty, but amateur skills suffice to build smaller works of equal beauty.

To really understand that glow, however, you have to do the job yourself. Lift the stones, fit them, turn them, and wiggle their bottoms into the yielding mortar. Only then can you touch the wall at the end of the day, feel its mass and know that the wall, at least, is there to stay—just exactly where you put it—and that it is a good wall. That is the essence of being an amateur anything: to do things for the joy of it and to enjoy the thing you have done. Whether or not one is trained, certified and duly paid are wholly irrelevant questions. It is the doing of it that really matters. A hired mason might give you a

somewhat more professional wall, but he cannot give you the joy of it.

Building with stone is not that hard to do. Not in a technical sense, anyway. Physically, there is a great deal of effort required. But the brain and the soul can find such work quite restful. The method, the process of putting stone upon stone, is as simple as the ancients who devised it. The technical mumbo jumbo that makes us shy away from doing such simple work ourselves is a latter-day deception. We've regressed from the unjust creed that some of us should not *have* to work with our hands to the even more absurd belief that most of us in the specialized technoconomies are no longer *able* to work with our hands. That is ridiculous. And yet we do it all the time. My favorite physicist decided he could figure out how to tune his own car only after learning that the high school dropout he had been paying to do the job had spent all of half a day in training.

Even closer to home was our own introduction to masonry. We had a city house with crumbling basement walls. I hired a mason over the phone—a name recommended by a friend. The mason had an Italian name—a fact that seemed comforting at the time—and he seemed to be familiar with the symptoms as I described them. We set the date, and he asked me to have all the materials delivered. That seemed a strange way for a highly recommended contractor to do business, but I didn't protest. He, after all, was the mason—not I. So I ordered up the requested amounts of sand, cement and sealabonda (which the first two suppliers I phoned had never heard of and which the third suggested might be Sealbond, a brand-name lime product). On the appointed day, I took a day off from the office and sat down to wait for the contractor's crew to arrive. I was looking so hard for the trucks and equipment that I didn't see the smallish gentleman step off the Number 7 bus. Even as he introduced himself at the door, I was looking over his shoulder for the rest of the troops. I mean, a basement is a big and complicated job, is it not? He carried his trowel in one hip pocket and his lunch in the other. Could he borrow, please, my shovel to mix the cement? His skills lived up to his reputation. No question of that. It was the *task* that my bureaucratic mind had exaggerated. The task was basic, obvious and simple even to me . . . after I saw him do it.

Much like laying stone: a bed of mortar, a mosaic of stones, more mortar, more stones. At the end of the day, there's another foot of wall. Touch it. Watch the shadows grow across it. Wonder how the world will change around it. Look again in a day or a year, and marvel that the wall still stands, just the way you made it. With any luck, Hazel, the house will never be done. Not as long as the joy is in the doing.